IT'S YOUR TIME TO SOAR!

FIVE STEPS TO TRANSFORM YOUR LIFE

By
MATTEEL D. KNOWLES, Ph.D.

It's Your Time to Soar!
Copyright © 2022 Matteel D. Knowles, Ph.D.
Published by West Oak Lane Publishing, LLC
Greenville, SC

All rights reserved.
No part of this book may be used or reproduced in any manner whatsoever without the written permission of the publisher.

ISBN: 979-8-218-14396-1

Disclaimer

Although the author/publisher has made every effort to ensure that the information in this book was correct at press time and while this publication is designed to provide accurate information in regard to the subject matter covered, the author/publisher assumes no responsibility for errors, inaccuracies, omissions, or any other inconsistencies herein and hereby disclaim any liability to any party for any loss, damage, or disruption caused by errors or omissions, whether such errors or omissions result from negligence, accident, or any other cause.

This publication is meant as a source of valuable information for the reader, however, it is not meant as a substitute for direct expert assistance. If such level of assistance is required, the services of an expert professional should be sought.

In loving memory of

Mrs. Mary Jo Groomes

DEDICATION

I dedicate this book to all the people who never had a chance to tell their stories.

I Am From

I am from back-alley steamed entrances, from downstairs workers for the people upstairs, from women who smelled good and wore slips and girdles beneath their dresses, and hats on their heads when they went to church—and who played the numbers, and took a little sip to take the edge off their nerves. I am from ducking in the car before going inside the house because the police were chasing someone on the roof. I am from subway and trolley rides to downtown, and bus trips to Broadway, and Aunt Kitty picketing because they messed with her retirement money after she lost her breast to cancer. I am from basements with washing machine rollers and washboards, and a dog chained in the yard outside, and large kitchens with metal cups with handles that made the water from the glass grapefruit juice bottle in the icebox taste extra good and cold and nurturing... and comforting... and cleansing. I am from not liking chitlins from the first time I tasted them and never eating them again. I am from hopscotch and double-Dutch and "come in when the lights come on." I am from viola lessons and piano and community theater and Up with People performance. I am from gangs on the corner and a father who stood up to them. I am from a family with no college, but knowledge that far exceeded the creativity of their enemies. I am from three hot meals at a dinner table without hate. I am from life-sized paper mâché Harriett Tubmans and Black History moments that stopped momentarily when we came down South, but always continued at home. I am from artisans and linguists and chefs and murderers... and psychotics and believers, and phenomenal achievers who beat the odds. I am from never truly fitting in and being a little bit okay with that. I simply am.

Table of Contents

FOREWORD 1

PRELUDE: Pre-Transformation 5

ACKNOWLEDGMENTS 10

INTRODUCTION: I KNOW A LITTLE SOMETHING.... 12

CHAPTER ONE: THE BUTTERFLY EXPERIENCE 22

SECTION I

CHAPTER TWO: I NEVER LOOKED BACK 33

CHAPTER THREE: FLIP YOUR MINDSET 40

SECTION II

PHASE TWO: The Caterpillar Molts 72

CHAPTER FOUR: I THOUGHT I WAS READY 77

CHAPTER FIVE: LEAP INTO ACTION 83

SECTION III

PHASE THREE: Pupa ~ Chrysalis 105

CHAPTER SIX: WHAT GOES AROUND COMES AROUND 109

CHAPTER SEVEN: YIELD TO THE PAIN 115

SECTION IV

PHASE FOUR: Adult Butterfly 143

CHAPTER EIGHT: Round Up! 146

CHAPTER NINE: COMPLETE YOUR PROCESS 153

SECTION V

PHASE FIVE: The Butterfly 169

CHAPTER TEN: Gives Me Chills 174

CHAPTER ELEVEN: SOAR! 181

My Incredible Journey: Soar! 196

CONCLUSION 197

Transformation 198

CHAPTER TWELVE: THE BUTTERFLY ON TOP 201

APPENDIX: DISCUSSION QUESTIONS 207

REFERENCES 209

ABOUT THE AUTHOR 210

FOREWORD

When I joined a major corporation over three decades ago (seems like yesterday), I decided, then, that I did not want to *achieve* the "silver milestone award." This award was a grandfather clock. Now, a grandfather clock is perfectly okay when it is a gift of choice. Somehow, the awarding of this unmoving object which occupies a relatively large space seems daunting—almost cold, if I may say. But the *executives* thought this gift was a perfect representation of 25 years of dedication. Just think for a moment... 25 of one's best years and a "grandfather clock" is representative of the time spent "clocking in and clocking out." I knew then, as I watched my first "silver anniversary," that I was going to learn all I could and exit before the clock struck "25 o'clock." No, I did not have a plan. I just knew I would not be present for my "silver endowment."

So how does this story relate to this book about transforming your life? In EVERY way!

The year was 2015. A mutual friend explained that I had so much in common with someone he knew and thought it would be a *sin* were we not to meet. We did, and I'm glad he was persistent, as we lived in different states. We "got together" and it seemed a new world was morphing from this first meeting.

Our first conversation lasted close to three hours (I knew because that's how long the charge lasted on my phone). From the inception, something inside affirmed that this would be no ordinary meeting. I discovered Dr. Knowles was in the early stages of one of her own personal transformation processes, and I was impressed at the level of commitment and total investment she was willing to make to embark on (and succeed) at this process. Talk about mindset change!

You see, we are all spiritual beings, linked in ways one cannot explain. Meeting Dr. Knowles was the beginning of the end of my corporate career as I knew it. She didn't know it, but the more we talked and worked on other projects, the more my desire to transition to other life passions grew. For example, I found myself volunteering more on global projects, and I developed an insatiable appetite to "change the world," or so I thought then.

The coming together of kindred spirits seemed to put order to how I volunteered. The more I volunteered, the more disconnected I became from the "kill and grill" world of corporate. My restlessness developed, and although I knew it was time to prepare to leave, I didn't know how.

In 2018, after gazing for hours at the pristine white snow on a gentle hill in the Midwest, I reflected on several life-affirming moments of "family first" that kept emerging at every twist and turn. I loved the people I worked with, but when it's time to *JUMP*, nothing can hold you back. I placed a call to Dr. Knowles. I'm not exactly sure of my exact words to her, but she understood that it was time for my "leap of faith." I wasn't scared, just unsure of how to make the transition. And that's just what my friend, Dr. Knowles, offered—a plan to make this as painless as possible. I WAS IN THE BUTTERFLY EXPERIENCE.

Without hesitation, Dr. Knowles (rather, my friend, Matteel), immediately volunteered to coach me through my transition. She very quickly had a suggested schedule and assignments for me. And so began my preparation to *JUMP*. Our conversations over the previous years definitely helped me "Flip *My* Mindset" (Phase One). What we worked on was the date I would "Leap Into Action" (Phase Two).

So where am I now? I am running my own company, registered in three countries and counting. All because a COACH assured me that I was on the right track, and she was right there with me.

In reading this informative, inspiring, game-changing, life-altering book, readers will get an honest, applicable process of action, faith, and "can do" to take the next steps into a life of fulfillment and purpose.

In her book, *It's Your Time to Soar!* Coach and Leadership Expert, Dr. Matteel Knowles presents the five phases in a meaningful way. Readers will experience a "coach in a book." The Butterfly Experience and the transformation process fill readers with hope, belief in self, and endless possibilities. It's a journey that allows readers to believe they can achieve their life's purpose by embracing the stages and allowing the universe to guide them along. Dr. Knowles, in writing *It's Your Time to Soar!* has certainly provided a manual that not only guides the reader, but BELIEVES HER AUDIENCE TO SUCCESS.

Effua McGowan, Author

The ABC's of Leadership

PRELUDE:

Pre-Transformation

A butterfly starts its life as an egg,
laid by a female adult butterfly after mating.
Butterfly eggs vary in size and shape,
and most are surrounded by a protective hard shell.

Story Time!

Ohhhh... HERE WE GO! Here we go!

EVERYBODY gather 'round!
Listen close to the sounds of my voice
While I tell you a story

No glory for me
Just gather 'round and hear
The wind intertwined in my words
That'd be the breath of your ancestors
Leanin' into every word I pray over you

You see, this story I'm about to tell you
Is like a prayer of hope
A prayer of life

It will grant you eyes to see
From whence we come

And when it get to the part

About the ocean

I want you to close your eyes

Real tight

And take a

Very

Deep

Breath

And tell me if every time

You don't smell

The salt of the sea?

Every time

COME ON CHILDREN!

Gather 'round close

That's right

Pull in real tight so you all can see

OH FATHER!

Pure glee forms at the corners of my mouth

When I just look at you

You are so beautiful

Glorious

Breathtaking

I want you to understand

All of it

Every morsel this way I can give

YOU

Back to you

Oh, how I want you to hear this tale

Come closer

Come a little closer

So I won't be too loud

Faces beyond the fire and the drums

Don't want us to gather

Ahhh… but I'd rather nurse the wounds of a beatin'

Than to keep this from you!

AHHHH... THIS IS A HAPPY DAY!

This passage

So rite for you

Bought with blood and tears and nursed with love

They cannot steal our minds

They cannot steal our souls

Lower the drums

The wind has spoken

And the time has come

Let us begin!

ACKNOWLEDGMENTS

I first thank God for His presence in my life and for His endless grace. I thank Him for the gifts and talents He has given me and for the life experiences He has allowed me to have. They have all been valuable.

I am thankful for the blood of my ancestors that runs deeply through my veins and warms my spirit. I am grateful for my parents, Dennis and Rachel, and my brother, Oren, for their honesty, love, and support throughout my life. I am thankful to my extended family, mentors, and dear friends—to everyone who believed in me, especially during the times in my life when I didn't believe in myself.

Finally, I could not have done this without my dream team. I owe a big *thank you* hug to my husband, Alex Knowles, who told me two years ago that my manuscript wasn't finished yet. He was right. I still had a lot more to say but didn't know it. I extend heartfelt appreciation to my writing coach, LaNette Kincaide of I Write Writing Academy, who guided my transformation from a casual writer to an author with a broad vision. Without a doubt, I know God sent you to me. Lastly, I thank my editor, Naomi V. Dunsen-White of Naomi

Books, LLC, for helping me breathe life into my book and teaching me how to refine my voice. God made sure they all showed up in just the right way and for reasons that extend far beyond this book. They have been my biggest sources of encouragement as I navigated my book-writing journey, and I am forever thankful for them.

INTRODUCTION

I KNOW A LITTLE SOMETHING

Real transformation means you never truly go back to the way things were. It permanently changes the very essence of who you are.

Eighteen years ago, Sonya was a 20-year-old single parent with a high school diploma and a five-year-old. At the time, she was working at the drive-thru window at a fast-food restaurant when a customer drove up to the window with her windshield wipers still on, drenching Sonya with water. Today, she's a homeowner, she's married, has a master's degree, and serves as a dean at one of the top universities in the country.

Shawna's life was turned upside down several years ago when she learned that her husband was abusing her child. A once joyful mother, wife, and volunteer with a budding career, she suddenly found herself blindsided by her church, her employer, and the criminal justice system. Fast forward 20 years—Shawna is now thriving as the Founder, President, and CEO of a non-profit organization dedicated to helping others transform their lives through anger management.

What do these two women have in common? They both encountered overwhelming personal challenges and overwhelming obstacles, but they took charge of their lives and rewrote their own stories.

You are the senior editor of your life story. Did you know that? Yes, God is the author. The devil is a liar, and YOU get to be the senior editor. That means YOU, my friend, have a say in how things go, in how you deal with all your stuff—the good, the bad, and the everything in between. We all go through life with *stuff,* and we all have goals, some sort of vision of the way we imagine our lives could go.

The difference is that some of us reach our goals, while others simply stay in that place of dreaming, wishing, hoping, and praying. There's a reason for that. I know that because I used to be the same way—dreaming about things, talking about goals, but never making it to the finish line to achieve any of the things I said I wanted the most. Thankfully, I figured it out! I figured out how to go from someone who just talked about my goals to someone who achieves my goals.

I don't think I've ever met anyone who doesn't have at least one goal. In fact, most of us have several—big goals, little goals, old goals, new goals; things we want to accomplish in different areas of our lives. So, if we take the time to have all these goals, then why is it that most people don't ever reach their goals? Yep, it's true. That's a real thing. Some people never even start, but even of those who start working toward their goals, most never finish. Some even get right to the point of almost finishing and then quit. It's not that they are bad people, or lazy, or do not want it badly enough. You can want something very badly and never achieve it. Unfortunately, it happens all the time. The challenge is that you either don't know how to get started, *or* you figure out how to begin but never get much beyond that point... and sometimes you repeat that cycle over and over and over again; going through life dreaming and talking about it. That can be so discouraging. Even more dangerous, it can cause you to believe things about yourself that just aren't true, like thinking you are a failure, or you are not capable of doing it. The truth is that you CAN do it, and you can do it with joy... with bells and whistles on. It's okay to win. It's okay to finish, and it's okay to feel happy and good about it. It's okay to SOAR!

I can say all of this with confidence because I have become an expert in transformation by reaching my goals again and again... more times than I can count, and the testimonies just keep coming. I'm not bragging. I am GRATEFUL. I am sharing. I want you to know that life really *can* be like this.

Yes, my life has come with plenty of ups and downs. That's just life. However, with God's help, I have mastered how to get from thinking about something I want to achieve, to doing it—whatever the "it" happens to be at any given time in my life. Now, I am going to share what I've learned with you. More importantly, I'm going to show you how to apply it to your life. I'm going to teach you how to finally, once and for all, get beyond your starting point, and keep going until you achieve your goals and experience the life you have always imagined. It all comes down to one thing: transformation.

Over time, I learned that any type of challenge I want to get through, or any type of goal I want to achieve, always, always, always... did you hear me say ALWAYS? It ALWAYS comes down to making some type of transformation. The Random House College

Dictionary Revised Edition defines *transformation* as: "[a] change in form, appearance, nature, or character."

Yes, what you're going to learn about in this book is dramatic and exciting because it is going to change your life forever! When I think about transformation and what it has meant in my life, I definitely think about it as being thorough and complete. In fact, real transformation means you never truly go back to the way things were because it's an irreversible inside job that permanently changes the very essence of who you are. I am so blessed to have experienced that type of lasting change many times.

Of course, I don't know everything there is to know about life and I never will, but I *do* know a little something... okay, I know a LOT about transformation because sooo many areas of my life have been defined by it in ways that changed me completely. For example, I went from starting my career in roles serving executives as their administrative assistant, and now I work as a senior vice president at a college and have an administrative assistant of my own. I was the first in my family to go to college, and I kept going until I earned a PhD. For 17 years, I was in an unhealthy marriage. I chose to get a divorce, and a few years ago married the perfect partner for me. After years of being on what could best be described as a genuine (but all over the place) Christian journey, I finally publicly proclaimed Christ as my Lord and Savior through baptism as an adult and landed at a home church that is the perfect fit for my husband and me. I have also gone through what might be the most profound transformation of my life to date—weight loss, having lost 180 pounds, naturally, within a few years.

So, yes, I know a lot about transformation because I have lived it and I practice it. In this book, I share what I've learned with you. I give it all to you, without holding back, because I also know what it's like to feel stuck, to never hit your goals and live the life you imagine—the life God planned for you. I desperately want you to experience what it feels like to make it, to live within your purpose, to stop just talking about it, and experience the tremendous benefits I have been blessed to enjoy because of learning how to transform my life.

To make *real* lasting changes, you do not just "add water and stir." There is a real method to transformation, and you need to know what you're doing. To teach it to you, I break it down into steps. I have been an educator for over 25 years, so what did I do? Yep, you guessed it. I created a model—a conceptual framework, if you will. In this book, I share that model with you by breaking down the five steps necessary for any type of real transformation. By the time you finish reading this book, you'll have all the tools you need to completely transform any area of your life, no matter how big or small, in good times and bad.

Once you learn the tools for transformation and how to apply them, no one can take them away from you. You will be able to apply the steps to any goal you set, but sometimes life will happen in ways that require you to transform without warning; and you'll need to know what to do and how to do it.

I have learned that it's even more important to be equipped with these transformation tools for those times when life hits you with a blow and the going gets tough. For example, I recently met a mother of four who lost a son to gun violence. That sounds horrific and inconceivable, right? Well, as if that weren't enough, the same woman had already lost another son in the exact manner six years earlier. However, to be in her presence, you would never know she had experienced such a tremendous personal tragedy. That's because she completely transformed her life in profound ways that allowed her to overcome what any parent would deem unthinkable. After her first son was murdered, she devoted her life to guiding others in their Christian walk and eventually began to offer grief support. Today, she's an entrepreneur running a successful childcare business.

Although she had not planned it, her goal was survival. That was her goal. It wasn't to run a marathon, start a fashion line, or write a screenplay. She was just determined to hold it together and not lose her mind. Thankfully, she did that through her faith and by working the transformation steps, even in the midst of personal horror.

I also know of a family whose mother and father (hard-working, first-generation immigrants) both passed away prematurely and unexpectedly within a two-year period. Although the siblings were adults when the parents died, this type of uprooting at the family's foundation could have completely changed the trajectory of their lives in devastating and irreversible ways, but it didn't. The entire family transformed into new versions of themselves. In fact, all three grown children maintained emotional balance, focused on their individual goals, and went on to transform their lives in ways that are pretty darned impressive to the average person. They would have made their parents proud. They have successful careers, solid marriages, healthy children, home ownership, business ownership, and incredibly strong family ties with newly established traditions. The goal was to save this family, and they accomplished that.

What all these stories have in common is that the people involved were determined to succeed, to make it, to become the best version of themselves… but that's not all. They did the work. When we hear about amazing tales of survival and accomplishment, we usually don't hear about what happened between the initial challenge and the triumph… but there's a lot that happens in between. In fact, that is where the heart of transformation lies—in the in-between stuff—in the pushing through. All the people in these stories took very specific steps to transform their lives and experience the type of existence they had desired and imagined—even in the face of personal tragedy.

Sometimes transformation results from an exciting goal you've had for years, and other times, transformation may be the result of something unexpected in life. No matter what it is for *you*, I know you are capable of making the changes and reaching your goals. I BELIEVE in you, but I am going beyond just believing in you and feeling good about what I know you can do. I'm going to teach you. I'm going to coach you through it and empower you, so you will have what you need to transform any area of your life.

You can do it. In fact, let's do it together. Let me help you.

If you're ready to soar, your wings are waiting.

CHAPTER ONE

THE BUTTERFLY EXPERIENCE

That butterfly can literally never again return to life as a caterpillar.

It becomes a completely new creation.

<u>I've Got Butterflies</u>

When I was cleaning and tidying my home office the other day, I looked around and realized just how many butterfly keepsakes I have collected over time. Some I've bought on my own, but because I talk about butterflies so much when I give keynote speeches or lead workshops, I have also received many as gifts.

It's not just that I think they're cute or pretty. I mean, after all, they're basically bugs. They start off as little creepy, crawly things that drag along on the ground, so that's not it. I love butterflies because of what they represent.

Nature offers us so many examples of complete transformation, and one of my favorites happens to be the transformation that a caterpillar goes through to become a butterfly. People frequently reference this metaphor when talking about transformation. I see it a lot in Christian literature and on social media, but I am personally inspired by it because it is so consistent, so complete, and offers so many lessons.

The Butterfly Experience Model

The process of the caterpillar's transformation leads to something breathtakingly beautiful that can flutter and soar to new places. A butterfly *used to be* a caterpillar. "Used to be" is important to note, because that butterfly can literally never return to life as a caterpillar. Those days are gone—ga' gone gone!

The caterpillar becomes a completely new creation, having new experiences and seeing things in a whole new way from a whole new vantage point. It truly represents what God does in our lives—makes us into new creations.

I created a model to present the required steps in any type of transformation, and I named it "The Butterfly Experience." It is a five-step process that, when followed, results in complete and permanent change.

The first step: "Flip Your Mindset"

The second step: "Leap Into Action"

The third step: "Yield to the Pain"

The fourth step: "Complete Your Process"

The fifth and final step: "Soar!"

The length of time needed for each step will vary, depending on the person and the goal, but it is important to work through each step without skipping any of them. Each step builds your transformation muscles to prepare you for the next.

The Butterfly Experience

- Flip Your Mindset
- Yield to the Pain
- Soar
- Leap Into Action
- Complete Your Process

MATTEELSPEAKS

The first three steps ("FLY") of The Butterfly Experience model involve major action on your part, while the last two steps still require your effort, but are designed to propel you toward enjoying the fruits of your labor. Each step is distinct and necessary for your complete transformation, so I break it all down for you in the upcoming chapters.

I discuss each step, in comparison to the caterpillar's transformation into a butterfly, and I demonstrate to you how I used the steps in my own life transformations. I also share some examples from the lives of real people who followed the steps and changed their lives, just like you will as you learn to apply these steps to your own life and live out your dreams.

If you're wondering why there must be steps or why there must be so *many* steps, please remember that *real* change, that really matters in your life, does not just happen. Even God created the world one piece at a time. The Bible says He first created the heavens and the earth. Then He added light. That was Day One. Then He made the firmament and separated the waters. That was Day Two... and so on, and so on, until you and I existed... and beyond. So, in the beginning (literally), God was modeling for us the wisdom of order, proper timing and patience, putting in the work, and building until you have what you envisioned "in the beginning."

It's certainly like that with the steps in this transformation model. Working through each step will prepare you for the next. So, I encourage you to appreciate each part of the model because there is a purpose behind each of the five steps—a reason for everything I'm telling you to do. I know from personal experience, and the experiences of others, that this really *does* work, and you don't have to figure it out on your own because I am here to help you.

Self-Reflection and Personal Discovery

This book is for YOU. It is designed, not only to inspire you, but guide you along your journey of personal discovery and transformation in one or more areas of your life. For that reason, you will notice I have provided a list of "Wing Tips" at the end of each of chapter.

The Wing Tips are there to assist you by offering an opportunity for you to slow down for some self-reflection time as you think about what you just learned and prepare for the next chapter. I have also provided a list of discussion questions at the end of the book to help you get started on your journey.

SECTION I

PHASE ONE:
The Caterpillar Hatches

A caterpillar develops within the egg and then eats its way out of the shell. This phase of the butterfly's life cycle is called, "larva."

Wrap Your Mind Around That

Wrap your mind around the idea of things not falling apart

Of your plans actually working out

And taking root

And sprouting

Into a life enriched

With desire

And needs fulfilled

Every

Single

Day

And spreading

And growing

And sowing seeds of happiness

And joy

And deeply rooted pleasure

In the lives of others

Through a regular harvest

Of that given and received

Wrap your mind around the gift of never tiring

Of your circumstances

And romance

Framed around the art of a normal life

No strife

Or deceit

Or ungluing of a feeling of permanence

And stillness

And home

Wrap your heart around the idea of giving and receiving amazing love

Mandated from above

Embrace the idea of spine-tingling touches and kisses that you feel

All the way down to the tips of your fingers

And the curve of your spine

And the curl of your toes

Wrap your spirit around the praising of your God

Every

Single

Day

For the rest of your life

Warmly enveloped in His protection

And guidance

And refreshing

And restorative

Indescribable love

Wrap your mind around *that*

CHAPTER TWO

I NEVER LOOKED BACK

I existed in a constant state of being stepped over and almost stepped on.
I blended in with my surroundings and just crawled around in circles.

How long had he been gone now? Six hours, eight, ten? I know he had left early that morning, and now it was evening. I had been here before, not literally the same location, but I had been here before—allowing myself to be mistreated just to be able to say I had a man—just to be able to fill the time during the lonely weekends. I would leave work on a Friday afternoon, all packed and ready to drive a couple of hours down the road to spend the weekend with the person I was dating. That gave me such an exciting answer when people would ask, "Got any exciting plans for the weekend?" It felt so good to be one of those people who could say that I did. I took pride in how adventurous it sounded, and I liked knowing that someone was waiting for me on the other end. Well, at least that was how it always sounded in the Black romance novels that featured sexy singles enjoying exciting weekend getaways.

Yet, no matter how much I tried to convince myself, this was not that novel. This was my feeling extremely tired at the end of a busy week at work, but ignoring my own need for rest. This was my ignoring the chores I would have normally done over the weekend and sometimes setting aside work I needed to bring home. I needed desperately to feel needed, desired, and wanted, which, at that time, meant having a man. I knew this person was not right for me when he was late to our very first date, but he was cute and I was desperate, so I put up with it. Now, when I say *late*, I don't mean running a little late. I mean me driving to a halfway point between where we both lived and waiting at the table for hours. I watched several other couples be seated, eat, and even linger over dessert and coffee, while I sat there waiting and making small talk with the server. I did not leave. I did not complain when he arrived. I just waited until he eventually arrived. It was a terrible sign… which I completely ignored.

So fast forward to a couple of months later. I continued to date him. I ignored the fact that he still had a very close friendship with his ex-girlfriend and her parents. I ignored his challenging relationship with his mother. Although it made me cringe each time, I ignored his use of a fake Latino accent to place his order whenever we ate at a Mexican restaurant. I ignored the fact that we were having unsafe sex, and I ignored that he had always been the loudest person in the room when I took him around my friends. The list went on… until it didn't.

You see, there I was waiting. It was a Saturday. I had driven the couple of hours to his house the night before. I didn't know he had business to take care of that weekend because he hadn't told me. All I knew was that I was coming for one of our weekends, and we would be meeting family for brunch after church that Sunday. Early that Saturday morning, we had sex, and he left with his truck and a trailer to do something in a city that was about an hour away. I passed the time by cleaning and tidying his house, and then I decided to surprise him with a homecooked meal. So, I went grocery shopping and even purchased some pots, pans, and dishes I would need. I prepared the meal, cleaned up, fed his dogs, and then I waited… and waited… and waited. Keep in mind, the city where he said he was going was where his ex-girlfriend and her family lived. But I was ignoring that, remember? He hadn't answered any of my phone calls or messages all day.

As midnight approached, I looked around the house of the person I was dating, where I had literally been sitting and waiting all day, and I realized that I'd had enough. We'd had so many fun experiences together, but something shifted in me, and I knew I deserved better than that. He knew I was driving in from out of town to spend the weekend with him, but there I was, sitting in his house alone for an entire Saturday.

I packed my bags. I didn't just pack the bags I had brought with me for the weekend. I packed everything I had gradually accumulated there during the past couple of months, and I got in my car and left. I texted one of my girlfriends to let her know I was hitting the road, so someone would know where I was and what I was doing; and I left. I drove away and never looked back… literally. I exchanged some text messages with him over the next day or so, but that was it. He blamed me and called me childish, but it didn't matter by then. I was done.

Now I know you might be asking how I could be so stupid to put up with all that, or you might be saying some version of "He knows he was wrong for that." However, the story isn't really about him at all. He's not the main character; I am. The story is about me finding *me*. If you think about it, nothing about the man in the story changed. His behavior is *his* behavior, but how I reacted to it is the point. That is where the metamorphosis happens. I wish I could say this had been the first time anything like that had ever happened to me. I wish I could say that was the first time I had ever put up with anything like that from a man, but it wasn't. This time period in my life was after I had divorced, so I had already lived through a 17-year, unhealthy marriage and had followed that with a series of unhealthy dating relationships. That was not the first time I had driven out of town every weekend to be with a man. That was not the first time I had packed all my stuff while he was away and left, never to return. I was broken and had not healed yet. I was at the bottom of the food chain when it came to dating. I was still a caterpillar.

Dating as a caterpillar was miserable. I existed in a constant state of being stepped over and almost stepped on. I blended in with my surroundings and just crawled around in circles. I didn't know any better. I thought that was how relationships worked because that was what I had endured for 17 years. I didn't realize I was never meant to stay down there that long, or that I was worth more, could demand more, and could live at a much higher level of being. I also didn't know I was already growing.

Being in a caterpillar stage isn't necessarily a bad thing, but you don't always realize what's going on with you while you're in it. In nature, a caterpillar forms after it is hatched from a very tiny egg. Then its job is to eat and grow—that's it. The caterpillar's job is to grow. In fact, it can grow to be 100 times its original size. That means when I'm in a caterpillar stage, I am designed to GROW exponentially! It means that is how God made me… to grow!

So, although I had been living my life and dating as a caterpillar that whole time, I was also growing but didn't even realize it. It took me several bad experiences to realize my growth, but I eventually did. I matured, and I grew, even during the time I was still a caterpillar. I grew through journaling and some other things I'll teach you about later. I also sought professional help during that time, and I worked through many of my unresolved issues with a licensed counselor. I was changing from the inside out, and I had begun to love, appreciate, and value myself in ways that were not dependent upon the love and approval of another person. Because I had "flipped my mindset," the way I saw myself had changed, and that *did* gradually affect the way the world saw me as well.

CHAPTER THREE

FLIP YOUR MINDSET

I didn't have a clear understanding of where things were heading.

I just sensed I was not supposed to remain where I was.

Flipping your mindset is the very first step in The Butterfly Experience, and let me go ahead and tell you... it is the hardest. This is the invisible part that nobody wants to think about or deal with, so they just glaze over it, sing, "la la la," and just try to skip it altogether. Many don't even know this step exists because most people who have made some type of major life transformation don't talk about it. It's not that they don't want to share it. It's just not the sexy part of hitting their goals. Still, they all did it, because you cannot transform in a complete and lasting way without it. It has to do with changing the way you see yourself, changing your mindset.

Think about it. What was a butterfly *before* she became a butterfly? She was a caterpillar on the ground, the bottom, and at her lowest point. It doesn't mean she lacks value and can't live out her life that way. It doesn't mean she's not loved and appreciated by family, friends, or employers, but the fact is, she was never designed to remain a caterpillar. God created her to be so much more. She just doesn't know it yet, but it is her destiny, her purpose in life—literally a part of her genetic make-up.

Living her life as a caterpillar, it is completely possible she might never have even seen a butterfly before because they exist in such different worlds. If she had ever encountered a butterfly, it may have never even occurred to her that *she* could become one herself. She was just down at the bottom, crawling along, doing her caterpillar thing, living her caterpillar life… but not her BEST life. All she sees around her are other caterpillars moving around in circles doing regular, everyday caterpillar things. At some point, that caterpillar looks up, feels the light on her chubby little caterpillar cheeks and begins to dream bigger and start believing for more. But more of what? Even without fully understanding what might happen in the end, she begins to feel a nudge in her spirit—a nagging desire for things to be different. Intuitively, she knows and believes in the possibility of something new.

This space of beginning to imagine yourself in a different way can be a tricky place for women who sense deep within that they are meant for more, but don't know what to do beyond that feeling. The reason it can be so tricky is that some women have lost all sense of hope. Their caterpillar experiences represent their bottom, and they stay there without being able to imagine a different experience. Sometimes you've believed in something so *many* times (and failed), that it's easier to just stop dreaming… also known as giving up. In contrast, for women who have figured out how to take back their mental power and give themselves permission to dream, that spot at the bottom represents an exciting new starting place, a new beginning—a place from which the only next step is UP. Isn't that exciting?

Just like in nature, no matter what, the caterpillar can only go UP from where she is, and that can only happen if she takes hold of the courage to open her mind to the possibility of a new experience. It can only happen if she starts dreaming again and imagining herself in a whole new way. She has to flip her mindset. Don't be afraid to close your eyes and imagine a new version of yourself, even if the picture is a little blurry at the moment. Just squeeze your eyes shut a little tighter and have faith that it can happen... that it WILL happen because you are in the process of learning how!

Renewing My Mind

My mindset flip started with my education. I was the first in my family to go to college and I kept going until I earned a PhD. However, my educational journey started long before the PhD classes. I say that because it started from within. After high school, I enrolled at a community college and started taking classes without any specific goal in mind. I had been a solid high school student who was very engaged in school activities, yet I lacked direction, social skills, and the kind of passion and momentum that come from having a solid dream and remaining laser focused on it.

At that time in my life, my self-esteem was not the best. I did not feel attractive, had never seriously dated anyone, and was preparing for a life of simply going to work, staying afloat as a responsible adult, and paying bills. I didn't know what I wanted to do with my life, and I clearly wasn't dreaming about any particular career, or a life filled with joy and passion. I was aimlessly going through the motions of taking college classes and preparing for adulthood.

As I hit my mid-twenties, I continued along with this pattern in my life. I worked in office jobs during the day and took college classes at night, but I never earned a degree. I realize now that I was just going through the motions during that time, feeling numb and robotic.

Ironically, when people interacted with me, they usually assumed I already had a college degree. I recall often feeling a bit ashamed when I had to correct them and explain. I felt those same feelings whenever I completed some type of application and selected "some college" where it asked for information about my educational background.

I went on like this for years, throughout my twenties and early thirties. Then I met Jo. Jo was my boss when I worked at a community college as an executive assistant. She was the Vice President for Student Development. I truly enjoyed working for Jo because I had a private, comfortable office on the second floor of the administrative building. I could focus, be creative, and support her leadership with a sense of confidence and pride in my work. She allowed me to spread my wings and try new things without fear of consequences if I failed.

Even with all those day-to-day experiences, the most valuable part of our relationship was how she helped me flip my mindset. Many people lovingly referred to her as "Mama Jo" because of her generosity with time and her maternal mentoring style. When I started working for her, I still wasn't serious about finishing college, but Jo *informed* me that I would be returning to school. I laugh when I think about it now. I don't remember the exact conversation, but I certainly do not recall her presenting the prospect of my returning to college as an option. It was obviously a mandate.

What I recall is a feeling of knowing she believed in me, and that meant the world to me. Jo saw something in me that I had not yet seen in myself. She saw the butterfly when I still saw myself as an ordinary caterpillar. Recently, in response to my social media posting about completing a course for professional speakers, Jo posted, "I always knew you were going to do great things."

Having someone believe in you when you do not yet fully believe in yourself is a powerful feeling, and I have had the opportunity to return the favor on several occasions. One example that comes to mind is my friend Janice. Janice is extremely funny, comfortable in front of a crowd, and loves to encourage people. She's also a very spiritual person who grew up in the church and loves to fellowship and worship with like-minded believers. I saw something in Janice that let me know she would be a great public speaker, so we started talking about it quite often. At the time, I had a little graphic design side-gig business, so I designed business cards, fliers, and promotional items for her. As a result, Janice began to see herself as a professional speaker. She started to accept opportunities to speak at churches and other venues. As her confidence grew, she even incorporated her depiction of a hilarious, fictitious character, "Miss Pinky," who speaks in a Gullah dialect and dons a large curly wig with a vibrant outfit to match. Janice's journey as a speaker began by someone seeing something in her that she had not yet seen in herself.

Jo's belief in me lit a fire inside of me. I began to feel *different.* I started imagining myself in a new way. Like that caterpillar, I didn't have a clear understanding of where things were heading. I just sensed I was not supposed to remain where I was. Before I knew it, I had earned an associate degree, bachelor's degree, master's degree, graduate certificate, and a PhD. It all began with my adopting a new mindset, a new way of looking at myself.

I Had Begun to Look Upward

When I look back at the road toward that PhD, I understand how flipping my mindset about my education also helped me shift the way I thought about my career. When I first completed high school, I wanted to go to college to major in journalism. In fact, I wanted to be a broadcast journalist. I loved to write and had even won a small scholarship for a poem I had submitted in a local competition. However, at that time, people who had good intentions talked me out of pursuing that career. I could not think of anything that excited me as much as writing, so I just started taking a variety of general education college classes since I couldn't be a journalist.

While studying at the community college, I was employed as a student worker in an office where I supported an administrative assistant named Carol. Carol mentored me about the importance of always establishing a trade—something on which I could fall back and find a job, no matter what. I took her advice and started taking elective classes in secretarial science: typing, shorthand, dictation transcription, filing, etc. Surprisingly, I really enjoyed the classes and was good in all of them, especially typing and word processing.

Those skills allowed me to secure desirable office jobs in large companies, supporting insurance adjusters, department managers, high-level executives, and attorneys. I loved what I did. I did it well, was highly respected, and felt proud of my work every day. I was always working on developing my skills and had decided that executive level administrative support would be my career for life. I was actively involved in a professional association for administrative professionals and was committed to doing my part to advance our profession and open doors for others.

Then I went to work for Jo, and she had other plans for me. She started giving me opportunities to fill in when there were vacancies in other areas at the college. For example, I would either help or serve officially in an interim capacity while the administrators figured out who they would hire to replace the employee who had left. I didn't realize it at the time, but those opportunities were shaping my career and building my resumé. I *wanted* to help, and I enjoyed learning new skills and doing things that were different from anything I had ever done before. It was exciting and fulfilling.

Also, during this time, some of the other employees at the college were not so positive and would say things to me like, "I don't know why you let them use you that way." I never saw it *that way* because my mindset had already begun to flip. I was already beginning to see myself in ways that were different from anything I had ever experienced before.

I saw myself beyond my executive assistant desk—not "better than" but surely different. I had begun to imagine myself as someone who could have her own private office with an assistant, business cards, and responsibility for a critical part of an organization.

When I reflect on that time in my professional life, I now understand that not everyone around me had the capacity to see my work experiences the way I did. What they viewed as an exploitation of my knowledge, skills, and abilities was merely an indication of their limiting beliefs. It wasn't their fault. We were all caterpillars at that time, and I may have felt the same way if the tables were turned. I had begun to look upward by then, so my view was already different. I am so grateful I did not allow others' limiting beliefs to penetrate my mindset and stunt my growth.

Those early seeds of being exposed to other types of jobs resulted in my eventual move into leadership roles at that college, and then on to my first vice presidency position at another institution. After that, I accepted a senior vice presidency role at a larger college in a larger city. Each of those life-transforming butterfly milestones was fueled as a result of my being open to dreaming and seeing myself in new ways.

I Realized I Was Worth More

Learning to think differently and change from the inside out helped me in other areas of my life as well. I got married when I was 27 years old. I married someone in November whom I had met in February of that same year. Before I knew it, it felt like I had blinked my eyes and awakened in a whole new world. I had moved several hours away from all my family and friends to a brand-new city and got married... just like that—in the blink of an eye.

In retrospect, when I am completely honest with myself, I knew things weren't quite right in the relationship from the very beginning, even before we got married. The signs were there in the (literal) little black book I had found among my then-fiancé's belongings. The book contained names and phone numbers of other women. The signs were there in the heavy *social* drinking at social events, and in the fact that I paid for my own engagement ring. At that time, I did not have the self-esteem, courage, or dating experience to recognize and acknowledge those glaring signs. I realized later that I was at a point in my life where I felt it was *time* for me to get married, so I ignored all the warnings and got married.

Marriage often has a way of not being exactly what you expected, even in the best of marriages, but it quickly became evident that things were going to be very different from what I could have ever imagined. Because the womanizing, partying, and heavy drinking continued, I spent a lot of time completely alone. I was very unhappy early in the marriage, but I was a committed wife, so I stayed and did my part to try to make it work. However, the constant drama that came with that type of dysfunctional lifestyle took a heavy toll on my emotional well-being, and I allowed it to break my spirit.

Over time, I became increasingly numb to the things that were happening in my life, and I used food to push down my feelings through compulsive overeating, isolation, and excessive busyness with work and school. Although I always maintained a big smile in public, my personal life had gone completely to hell, and my self-esteem issues worsened throughout the 17-

year marriage. Already obese at 5'2" and 242 pounds when I married, I gained another 110 pounds during the course of that marriage, weighing in at 352 pounds.

However, because I was also attending college during most of that marriage and was experiencing success in my career, something slowly began to churn deep within me, and that something minimized the negative impact of my detrimental relationship. I was beginning to remember I was worth more... a lot more.

I also had to acknowledge that I was very unhealthy in just about every way—spiritually, mentally, and physically. No longer willing to sacrifice my health and sanity to preserve my public and covenant commitment to persevere in marriage, I sought a divorce.

My mindset had flipped completely. The *old* me had been lying to myself for years about the harsh realities of my marriage. I had grown comfortable living that lie and had cosigned an unspoken agreement to pretend. That showed up as calling the police because my husband hadn't been home in a couple of days; finding his car at another woman's house at three o'clock in the morning with his wedding band in the cup holder; losing my cherished viola because he threw it across the room in a drunken rage; picking him up from the police station after he was caught driving with a suspended license; him denying me sexually and telling me that I was more of a turnoff than a turn-on; or turning around and returning home on the way to church because he was too hungover, and we had to keep pulling over so he could vomit. These things (and so many more) had become my normal—just part of another day, like adding cream to my coffee every morning.

After 17 long years of this craziness, something new had finally begun to stir and awaken inside of me. By the grace of God, I began to imagine a life where I could be free from drama and be happy and healthy. Although I believe strongly in marriage, seeking a divorce turned out to be one of the best decisions of my life. It was one of the first times in my life when I put *my* needs first, even though it was scary. There were so many reasons why I could have talked myself out of it. I was living several hours away from any family, so I was alone. My husband lost his job, and was angrily sitting around the house without any sense of direction, so I had to face the judgment of others about my timing. Although I was making a decent salary as a college vice president, we had a mortgage on a $338,000 house, a car note, credit cards, my student loans, his child support, the other usual bills, and we only had about

$5,000 in our savings account. So, I wasn't sure if I would have enough money to cover everything. I was also still in school working on my PhD and had an intensely busy, full-time executive-level job. It was a very overwhelming time.

Despite these realities, a new version of me had begun to emerge as a result of my having experienced so many incredible transformations in other areas of my life. That *new* me no longer aligned with being mistreated and overlooking it. That *new* me no longer aligned with a victim mentality. Every single college degree I had earned had come with some type of sacrifice, something that had required me to dig down deep to stick with it and make it to the finish line. Going through experiences like that (time and time again) had rebuilt my stamina, determination, discipline, and self-worth; and all those things strengthened my confidence to do what I needed to do to free myself from the unhealthy relationship.

Therefore, when it came time to make the decision about divorce, it felt as though the decision had already been made, and I was just catching up with it. I remember sitting on my bed one morning and writing down all my thoughts and feelings. I felt calm and centered, not weepy or nervous. I wrote a multiple-page letter and gave it to my husband so I wouldn't forget even one thing I wanted to say. Today, I don't even remember what was in that letter, but I know it marked the beginning of the end of our marriage. I knew the road ahead would be eventful and long, but I felt a peace I had not felt in years.

Years later, I can honestly say it was all worth it. I have married the perfect partner for me, and I am so thankful for that. What I realize, though, is that the relationship is different because I am completely different.

Because of everything I went through and because of *how* I went through it, I now show up in my healthy marriage as a woman who knows I deserve to be treated well. I show up as a woman who values myself enough to communicate my needs, even when the conversation is uncomfortable. I feel like a completely different human being—completed and transformed.

Because I didn't skip any of the steps of the transformation experience, I was able to move through the process of divorcing, healing, and transitioning into a new relationship in a healthy way. I'm not saying it was always easy or pretty, but I definitely came out on the other side of my first marriage without feeling bitter, without wishing my ex-husband any harm, and without behaving poorly toward him or others. I had completely transformed into a butterfly version of myself, ready to love another human being as much as I had learned to love myself!

I am watching a friend go through a similar situation right now, and I can tell she's in the process of shifting her mindset. I will call her, "Melba." Melba has been married for many years and she and her husband have children. She recently shared with me that she is currently grappling with the decision of whether she should stay in her marriage or leave. She has sought professional counseling and speaks of her value and the spiritual transformation she is currently experiencing. That ultimate decision is hers to make, and it is not my place to influence it. I want her marriage to work, but I will support her as a friend no matter what she decides. No matter how things go, I want her to be a woman who is whole, healed, loves herself, and knows she deserves to be healthy and treated well.

Transformed by the Renewing of My Body

When it comes to this idea of flipping my mindset, nowhere in my life has that been more evident and impactful than in my weight-loss journey. Since childhood, I have always been somewhere between chubby, thick, overweight, or morbidly obese. No matter how you want to label it, I was fat. There's nothing fundamentally wrong with being fat because we come in all sizes, but for a very long time, I was physically unhealthy. I was always on the verge of developing diabetes, but I didn't have it. I was always on the verge of developing high blood pressure and eventually did. When I walked, I was short of breath, and my cholesterol was high. I no longer fit well inside my car; my arms squeezed against the inside of the door and the armrest, and I could barely close the seatbelt. I always had to request a seatbelt extension when I flew on an airplane. I'm pretty sure I had developed sleep apnea because I sometimes awoke with the sensation of drowning and gasping for air. Although I didn't openly acknowledge all these things to myself while I was experiencing them, I was undeniably unhealthy.

I had lived that way for so long; it had become my normal existence. There were times in my life, especially as an adult, when I decided to embrace my body size and celebrate it, because I was learning how to think more positively about myself and love myself no matter what. There's absolutely nothing wrong with self-love and self-esteem.

My looming health risks were still very serious, but it was critical that I loved myself from the inside out. It was critical that my limiting beliefs had begun to fall away, and I was learning to love and appreciate the person I saw when I looked in the mirror. It was essential for me to grow into that mindset before I could love myself enough to want to take care of my whole self—body, mind, and spirit. Because I was no longer numb to the realities of my unhealthy ways, I cared. I cared about my existence and my purpose. I knew I could no longer just glaze over and ignore those looming health issues. I knew the risks would eventually catch up with me, so I had to do something about it.

Well, I *did* do something. I will talk more about that in the next chapter, but long before doing something about it, I began to want it. I began to want it badly. I started dreaming about becoming a different version of myself—a healthier version. I thought about what I would look like and feel like as I prepared to go to bed every night. I purchased magazines that featured women on the cover who had lost 100 pounds or more. I went to a counselor and a life coach. I created vision boards with images of what I wanted to look like. I flipped my mindset by getting into dream mode and fantasizing about reducing my health risks, how my body would look, and how I would feel.

I began to love myself more at size 28, the largest size available at most plus-size women's clothing stores. I felt grateful because I had learned to appreciate myself no matter what. I realized I could not hate myself and love myself at the same time, so I chose love. I bought nice clothing and was always well-groomed because I needed to look in the mirror and see someone I admired, not hated. I loved myself enough to get healthy.

In addition, I did not want to be the stereotype. I was big, female, and African American with a family history that includes heart disease, diabetes, cancer, and more. I knew those things were eventually going to catch up with me, like a game of Russian roulette. So, I started thinking about what life would look like if I were not just existing, but thriving and trying to avoid chronic disease. Instead of thinking about health and wellness as something that was for other people and other cultures, I started imagining a life where I would be exercising regularly, and preparing and eating healthy food. I shifted my mental focus to one of embracing LIFE, not simply avoiding DEATH.

New Mindset - New Tribe

So, what does it really mean to breathe life into your goals by flipping your mindset? Like that caterpillar who had not yet become a butterfly, you must have that *thing* in you that can dream without limits.

Get yourself around positive people who have done what you want to do, and then allow them to influence you—like I did with Jo, who influenced my education and career. Even if you cannot see it yet and do not really feel it or believe it yet, start by trusting the people around you who see something in you that you don't yet see in yourself. I know for certain that God sends people to guide us and help us, but we must let them help us without resisting them or sabotaging their genuine efforts. Yes, flipping your mindset often begins with a feeling, but it is so much more than that.

Flipping your mindset sometimes means it's time to take stock of those around you. Who are they? Are they enhancing your life or are they bringing you down? Are they adding any value, or are they usually talking about something negative or gossiping about how other people are living their lives?

You almost need to think about it as though you are the Chief Executive Officer ("CEO") of your own destiny (your own life), and the people around you serve as your personal board of directors. You would not have people on your board who can't do their job in a way that's going to help your company reach its goals. You have to think of yourself in that same way, and that means you might need to hire some people and you might need to fire some people.

Pay attention to who you need in your circle because it truly affects the way you think. Without a doubt, you need people around you who not only genuinely care about you but also have knowledge, skills, and abilities in areas where you have little or no experience or success. If you're bad with money, get someone around you who is good with money. Allow them to mentor you and change the way you think about money. If you have always wanted to lose weight, get around someone who has a great track record in that area, and accept his or her help. If you're not good at networking and meeting new people, there are always people who are amazing at that. Reach out to them. They will help you. In fact, people like that LOVE to help other people connect. It's part of what lights their fire, so don't be afraid to ask because it will probably help them too.

As CEO of your life, you will also have to do some firing. There will be those from whom you will gradually need to ease away or eliminate from your circle of influence. This can be tricky because sometimes these people are close friends or even family. It doesn't mean you literally have to cut them out of your life if you don't want to (although sometimes that's exactly what's needed), but you may need to put a little distance between them and you, so they'll have less influence on your mindset. They may not understand, but it's okay, because you're learning how to put yourself first and worry less about what others think. Remember, just because you're flipping *your* mindset won't mean those around you will be ready to do the same, and that's okay, too. It doesn't necessarily mean they are bad people. However, it surely means *you* are growing.

People get used to your being one way, so the changes they see in you can be scary for them, which can make them feel uncomfortable. I pivoted from the standard American diet and began to eat like a vegan. People who weren't vegan would turn up their noses or make fun of my food while we enjoyed a meal together. Although I was minding my business and eating my food, some would look at my plate and comment, "That looks nasty" or "I have to have my meat." At times, it was clear people just had a natural curiosity that resulted in questions. For others, my choice to eat in this way just seemed to make them extremely uncomfortable. When I later returned to classic eating that included animal protein, I distanced myself from a group of friends who are passionate supporters of the whole food and plant-based lifestyle. Their reasons are grounded in their care about the environment, the community, and reducing chronic disease, but they continued to contact me with judgmental comments without ever asking me the reason for my change or asking me if I was okay.

The *old* me would have felt that I owed them an explanation, and I would have allowed their comments to leave me feeling ashamed and doubtful about my ability to make decisions about my own health and well-being. This new version of me felt the heat rise from the bottom of my feet to the top of my head as their comments hit my inbox, because I knew I didn't have to allow them to treat me that way. I didn't have to take it, and they didn't get to define me or influence my thoughts about myself unless I allowed them to do it... so I cut them off. They are good people and certainly a group I considered friends, but my need for self-preservation and a healthy mindset outweighed my need for those friendships and the negative energy associated with their opinions about my lifestyle.

Some people never have a positive thing to say about anything. People who only have the capacity to imagine bad outcomes in most situations simply must go. If you can't remove yourself from them, please remember that you are not required to share your plans with them. I promise you; they will not be supportive or encouraging anyhow. If you let them get into your head, you risk allowing them to halt your progress. If you allow someone else to halt your progress, you might never even get started for fear of what might go wrong.

Remember, we're still at the mindset part—the first step in a five-step process for transformation. We're not even talking about *doing* anything yet. That is how powerful the mind is. The reason I'm emphasizing this step so heavily is because it is truly the basis of any transformation journey. It provides the cornerstone that will support you through the ups and downs that will come. Do not skip the time to navigate this step. Transformation requires other steps, but it always, always, always must start on the inside. You must first *believe* you can achieve your goal and begin to imagine yourself getting there without allowing in any limiting thoughts and beliefs.

One of the most empowering things about being a butterfly is she gets to soar, explore, and go to greater heights. Imagine if that butterfly allowed herself to be influenced by others who got in her head and constantly told her she could never be more than a caterpillar. That would be the beginning of the end for her because it would be the equivalent of allowing others to physically hold her down on the ground, preventing her from rising to her greatness.

In life, some people are like that. Years ago, I worked with a woman named Robyn. Robyn was just negative. She thought she was a positive person, but I could tell within the first few seconds of saying, "Good morning," to her if it was going to be a "good Robyn day" or a "bad Robyn day." Robyn looked beautiful when she took the time to wear make-up and was in a good mood. On the bad days, she would skip the make-up, revealing dark circles beneath her eyes. She grumbled in response to my bubbly, "Good morning!" Most of Robyn's life circumstances were out of control: her money, her relationship with family, her vehicle, her home, etc. If I asked her for an update related to something about which she had previously seemed upbeat and excited, the response was usually negative. Immersed in gossip with other coworkers, Robyn always seemed to know about bad things going on within the organization and always seemed to feel victimized by whatever decisions the higher-ups made.

Stay away from the Robyns in your life… FAR away. They are dangerously unhappy. They don't expect you to be happy, and they will always be on standby to await your bad news. Run! If you have a lot of Robyns around you, it is highly unlikely you will be able to achieve your goals and obtain the life you want.

Manifesting the Mindset

I don't know the author of this quote, but it is one of my favorites: "If you believe it, you will achieve it." This means putting all your focus on what you want and envisioning yourself as though you have already achieved it. You can do this in many ways.

One manifesting method that has worked for me is using vision boards. Vision boards are creations on which you attach photos, words, and objects of things that represent precisely what you want. For example, I have certain body goals associated with my fitness activities, so I have photos of what my body will look like when I hit those goals.

Similarly, as I scale my business as a motivational speaker, I use photos of successful speakers on stage, along with images and other symbols that represent large audiences and international travel. My husband

and I have done the same thing with our dream house. We keep that vision board in a prominent location in our current home. We are believing in these things now, before we even see them or achieve them. We imagine ourselves walking around in the new, spacious home, entertaining family from out of town, cooking together in our kitchen and working out in our home gym. We already *see* it! It's already there. We don't even talk about it in any other way. We just have to catch up to it.

Post-it notes also work as a powerful source of personal affirmation to help shift your mindset. You may use simple post-it notes and write your goals, motivational sayings, favorite scriptures, or anything that represents your desires and keeps you feeling focused and inspired. Put these post-it notes everywhere—on your bathroom mirror, on the dashboard of your car, in your office, etc. Place them wherever you will see them on a regular basis, and periodically recite them aloud as well. Some people rehearse their affirmations every single morning as a way to start their day and embed those things into their psyche, which helps them begin to flip their mindsets.

You may also journal and write about your hopes, dreams, and plans. If you're not sure how to journal or what to journal, ask for help from a counselor, life coach, or someone else who has done it before. There are always people who have already done what you dream of doing. Find them, talk to them, and ask for their guidance. There are also websites to help you get started with journaling prompts. Smartphone applications are available that will guide you through a journaling process every single day. One of my favorites is the Gratitude app, where I can type my own daily affirmation in a designated place in the app. Plus, they automatically send me a new one every morning.

There are so many ways to flip your mindset, but doing the work to get crystal clear about what you want is critical. Surrounding yourself with positive people, doing things that keep your goals in front of you and get you excited about what you are going to achieve are just some of the tools available. This is how transformation begins from the inside out.

These approaches might feel a little awkward to you at first, but you *cannot* skip this step. It is imperative you put down solid roots because believing you can do it, keeping your energy bright, and *seeing* yourself doing it, are some things that will help you stand strong later and remember why you started in the first place. I promise you, there will be moments in your transformation journey when you are going to need that strength.

Wing Tips

My Incredible Journey: Flipping My Mindset

- What are my dreams and goals?
- What has kept me from achieving these goals in the past?
- What's holding me back now?
- Do I have a plan to reach my goal?
- Who are the people in my family and close circle of friends?
- Who is very positive, supportive, and always sees the bright side in any situation?
- Who in my life is always negative, no matter what?

- If I think of myself as the CEO of my own life, who do I need to add to my team (my personal board of directors) to be successful? Who do I need to remove?

- What are some positive affirmations that would help me daily?

- Can I imagine myself reaching this goal? Why? Why not?

- Why do I want to reach this goal?

- How will I feel if I never reach this goal?

SECTION II

PHASE TWO:

The Caterpillar Molts

A caterpillar spends all its time eating.
As it grows, the caterpillar becomes too large
for its skin and molts (sheds its skin).
Depending upon the type of butterfly,
caterpillars molt four or five times.

I Think I'm Ready

That full abandon type of trust
Stepping fully into it
Letting it get on me
Run through me
Cling to me
And cleanse and renew me

He might change my plan
Let Him

He might not understand
Tell Him
I'm afraid to accept His gifts
And open my fists and surrender
Into the tender arms of His loving
Guidance
And remembrance

And grace

Just let Him handle it

Just relax
And always remember that
He's got this

I don't have to be tired anymore
I don't have to try to fix it anymore
I don't have to remix it anymore
Trying to get a deeper color
To make it look pretty on my own

And I don't have to explain
Or re-frame my own life

Cause He already know

All I have to do is retrain my mind

And my body

And my spirit

Rundown and conditioned for a life of strife

To listen… and really hear

And reopen my heart

To experience a new life

But I'm scared

And it's rare that I'm out of control

But my soul cries for timely intervention

And a depth of relationship

Through reading and meditation

And clarification

Of what I'm supposed to do

What I suppose to do Lord?

Just tell me

Continue to compel me

To draw close to You

To hear You
And feel You
And really know You
And love you even more

And just let You handle it

I think I'm ready to get out of your way now
I think I'm ready to stand in the Son now
And allow your Spirit to fill all of my holes

CHAPTER FOUR

I THOUGHT I WAS READY

Just do it scared. Just do it nervous.

I recently attended the funeral of a beautiful, talented woman who had admittedly ignored a persistent cough until it was too late. By the time she went to the doctor to get it checked, she received the unfortunate news that she had stage-four lung cancer. Not every decision we put off results in literal death, and we don't know for sure if the outcome would have been any different if she had gotten help earlier; but her death certainly made me think about the consequences of my own actions… or lack thereof.

In just about every aspect of our adult lives, there are things we know we're supposed to take care of, and if we don't, things could go very wrong. This goes for our cars, our jobs, our physical health, buying Christmas gifts, saving money, and more. One of the worst feelings in the world is knowing you *could have* taken care of something. You had the time and the resources, but you just didn't get it done. For whatever reason, you just didn't do it.

One experience that still stings for me today is that I didn't take advantage of an opportunity I had to go on a mission trip to Haiti several years ago. I had scraped together enough money for the down payment, and I had the support of an international community service organization, of which I was a member. I would have been going with a group of people who had been before. They knew the lay of the land and had the connections in place to keep everyone safe. It was going to be a wonderful opportunity to serve, to grow, to stretch beyond my comfort zone… but I wasn't ready.

I thought I was ready. I was an active member of the sponsoring organization, and I was doing and saying all the right things. However, I allowed my fears to stop me. I allowed my own self-limiting beliefs to defeat me. For example, the organization is a long-standing, reputable part of the community, but the members are predominately White. While that has never been an issue for me as a member, I convinced myself that I was probably going to be the only Black person going, and I might be uncomfortable in that situation, especially in a predominately Black country like Haiti. Now, keep in mind, I didn't even know the races of the people going. Statistically speaking, they would probably all be White, but I didn't even know that for sure. More important, if they *were* all White, it had nothing to do with this mission trip, and I never had any negative experiences with any of the members of our chapter. I was literally making up concerns in my mind, and those concerns just continued to grow and fester.

Next, I started listening to a friend who had been in the military. I mentioned the upcoming trip and his immediate response was, "Ohhh, nooo. You don't want to go to Haiti." Then he began to share horror stories with me; horror stories of American missionaries who had been kidnapped in Haiti. He shared examples of extreme violence in Haiti and said that even he, with all his military experience, would never go to Haiti... *gulp*.

So, you know what I did. Yep, I backed out. I backed out of the trip. I don't even remember the reason I gave, but what made it worse was that I had convinced one of my friends to go and then *I* backed out. So, I wasn't just backing out on myself; I was backing out on a friend as well. I lied to myself and convinced myself it was okay because she was White, and because she was a more experienced world traveler.

Fresh out of my early caterpillar stage, I was attempting to take this step to do something new; to do something different, adventurous, and meaningful, but I did not have the guts to go through with it. It looked good on paper, sounded good when I said it aloud, but I had never been around anyone like me, with my background, who just went out of the country on a mission trip to a third-world country—especially with a group of White people they didn't know well. I wasn't mentally strong enough yet to try new things that were so far out of my comfort zone, and I didn't have the kind of people around me to support such a radical decision. I had people around me, but they were the ones who convinced me to stay put because it was safer. They were the people who gave me all the reasons why going on a mission trip to Haiti was a terrible idea. They were the people who expressed great relief when I told them I wasn't going.

Making the decision not to go on the mission trip to Haiti caused me to miss out. I will never know everything I missed, but I know I missed the opportunity to see a new country and help some people there. I know I missed the opportunity to be uncomfortable, face that feeling and overcome it. I know I missed the opportunity to become closer friends with the other volunteers from my organization, and I surely missed out on making new friends, experiencing a new culture, and possibly, establishing a whole new network.

I don't like to stay in a place of regret, of focusing on what I "would'a, could'a, should'a" done, but I *do* think it's important for me to get the lesson. In this case, the lesson for me is about how important it is to push through and take the necessary steps to do something new; to do something I've never done before, even if I have to do it scared. Thankfully, the friend I invited to go along still went and had a great experience, and I am thankful we are still friends today. But I clearly allowed fear to cripple me and stop me in my tracks. I know now that it is always better for me to take the steps, even baby steps, to move forward with something I know I should be doing, instead of putting it off. It might be something small, like starting my Christmas shopping earlier, so I'm not rushing in December. It might be something more important, like getting a medical check-up that I would rather avoid. What matters is that I take the leap, even if my legs are trembling.

Just do it scared. Just do it nervous. When I've done that, I have never regretted it, and even if it was a rough landing, I have always landed on my feet!

CHAPTER FIVE

LEAP INTO ACTION

You might fall.
In fact, you might fall multiple times,
but if you keep trying, you will eventually conquer that first step.

It's time to be about that business! Yep, it's time to get it. I mean REALLY get started, like "for real, for real," not just talking about it. Like my fitness coach says, "LET'S GOOOO!" I don't like those days when he's all perky and has that sparkle in his eye because it means he's *waaayyy* pumped up. That means I'm going to have to dig deep and work even harder, so I can take it to the next level and achieve the goal for that day. Yep, like most people who have a good personal fitness trainer, I have a love/hate relationship with mine, but I know it gets me where I need to be so I can accomplish what I set out to do at the very beginning.

The second step in The Butterfly Experience model is kind of like that. That's why it's called "Leap Into Action." It requires energy, momentum, and trust. The first step in the model requires a lot of mental energy, but this transformation journey is way more than a mental game. It's an uphill battle that you will win, but you're going to need to burn some calories along the way to get it done.

You see, once our caterpillar has flipped her mindset and started looking upward and forward at what could be, at some point she's going to have to get off the ground. She *has* to get up. That is the only way she's going to get going.

The tricky part is that she is used to being at the bottom. She knows how to do life down there. All her friends and family are caterpillars, and they're right down there with her, just living it up, living life. She has seen many others do just fine in their little caterpillar world. They seem happy and content enough, yet she still feels a deep longing inside for something more. She can either pay attention to that feeling and do something about it, or she can stay where she is and ignore it. The decision is hers to make—to do something or stay where she is. That's the choice. Since the feeling of being drawn to something different is so strong, at some point she must do more than simply look up and believe. She will have to take action. She will need to *do* something.

For our caterpillar, taking this first step means climbing up onto a branch where she has never been before to begin her journey toward something she has never even experienced... becoming a butterfly. Remember, she must take this step even though she may have never seen a butterfly before, or even heard of one. She just senses that something better awaits, and she feels like she must go for it, so guess what she does? Even though she feels afraid, even though she feels alone, and even though she doesn't fully know what she's doing, she prays about it. She musters the courage to take a chance on herself, to believe in herself, and she does it. Knees trembling (yes, caterpillars have knees), she takes her first step.

A Taste of Success

Taking that first step can often be one of the scariest things you will ever do, no matter what your goal is. Even if it seems like something simple for others, it might terrify you. That's alright, and it is completely normal.

For example, many people feel excited about submitting an application for admission to a college or university, but for others, that excitement is replaced with a debilitating sense of dread and terror. I have spoken with students who applied to college, but later admitted they had been thinking about it for years before they took the first step and followed through with it. My friend Sonya said she thought about attending the local community college in her city for an entire year before she worked up the nerve to walk through the doors of the college, down the hall to the admissions office and let them know she was there to get started on a two-year associate degree. An entire year! Others admitted they had sat in their cars for hours before getting the nerve to walk into the building and speak with an admissions officer.

That's how scary it can be to take a first step when heading into new territory. Today, Sonya has a master's degree, but it all started with that first step. She had to get out of the car.

For me, getting serious about my education required me to shift from talking philosophically about going to college to taking all the steps necessary to become a college student and ultimately a college graduate. It was one thing for other people to believe in me and see something I may not have seen in myself, but at some point, I had to complete real, live college courses and meet all program requirements to earn a college degree.

It took a good kick in the behind to shove me toward my first step. It all started while I was working at that community college when Mama Jo informed me that I would be going back to school. After years of taking classes without any sense of direction or end goal in mind, this was the first time I had felt hopeful about college in a very long time. I didn't know it, but I just needed help from someone I trusted, admired, and didn't want to let down. I just needed someone to believe in me. When Jo made that declaration on my behalf, it felt like someone had grabbed me by the shoulders from behind with both hands, turned me in the right direction and gave me a big push. It turns out that was exactly what I needed to get on the path toward my goal.

I had been right there working in a college environment and had already earned about 110 credit hours at previous colleges and universities. Despite earning all those credit hours, I still didn't have any type of earned college credential. I was a good student with solid grades, but because I lacked a clear objective, I had just been taking random classes here and there and periodically changing my major. By that time, I had been taking classes at night for years. It was just what I did, and it allowed me to tell people I was "in college," although I wasn't progressing toward anything in particular.

It turns out I was only about 15 credit hours from earning an associate degree at the same college where I worked. So, I submitted an application, got accepted, completed those classes at night after work, graduated, and took part in the commencement ceremony to celebrate my accomplishment. I had *finally* finished something after all those years in school, and it felt amazing!

Once I got a taste of that success, the rest just flowed. It became easier each time to imagine myself obtaining the next degree, applying to the next college or university, taking the appropriate entrance exams, and figuring out how to pay the tuition. I had gained momentum, and I felt unstoppable. From there, I went on to earn a Bachelor of Arts degree in Counseling and Human Services; a Master of Career and Technology Education; a Graduate Certificate in Higher Education Leadership, and a PhD in Higher Education Administration from our state's flagship university. I had figured out how to do what was necessary to get started on whatever I wanted. I could hit that same start button in any other area of my life.

Getting Comfortable with Being Uncomfortable

When I think about leaping into action with my career, the opportunity to pursue my first vice presidency position stands out as a critical milestone along my journey to live a life of courage and trying new things, even if I felt afraid. At the time the job became available, I was still working at the college where I had experienced so much personal and professional growth. I felt safe there. I felt comfortable and could have imagined staying there for my entire career until I retired.

I started working at that college as an executive assistant to a vice president and had advanced into a role where I was responsible for all the college's enrollment services and led a team of professionals. I was in a prominent leadership position, making more money than I had ever made before. I had a nice, corner office with a wall of windows from the ceiling to the floor. I was still learning and growing through professional development opportunities, and I lived within walking distance of the campus. Although I was in the 14th year of a tough marriage, my professional life was comfy and "snug as a bug."

Then, someone contacted me with one of those "you would be perfect for this opportunity" phone calls. I had zero thoughts or intentions of making a move from my job then, much less becoming a vice president. Like the butterfly still on the ground at this stage, I was content with what I was doing and felt just as cozy and secure as could be. However, sometimes leaping into action requires you to get super uncomfortable. In fact, I'll go ahead and say it: it *always* requires that. You usually *have to* give up something, even if it's your sense of ease and familiarity.

Humans are creatures of comfort, not discomfort. So, what did I do? I ran, of course.

I tried to run from the opportunity by not responding quickly to calls from the friend who told me about the job. I talked to friends and family who encouraged me not to "give up a good thing" with my current job. When the prospective employer's human resource officer reached out to me to schedule an interview, I responded by letting her know that I unfortunately had something scheduled for each of the times she offered. *Really, Matteel? You couldn't reschedule anything in your life to accept an interview for the position of vice president at a college?* I was clearly scared to death, frozen in fear, and avoidance was my weapon of choice at that time.

I talked with my husband about how much better it would be not to uproot him from his job. If I got the job, it would require us to sell our house, quit our jobs, and relocate. I also rationalized that it wouldn't be a good idea to move four hours from my parents, who had recently retired and relocated to the same city where we lived. I came up with every reason under the sun for why pursuing the new job would be a horrible idea.

Despite my efforts to sabotage the opportunity, a mentor convinced me to go for it, so I did. Again, it was the little nudge from another person who believed in me that gave me the courage to take a very scary first step. You must remember, my caterpillar days had been in a support role as an administrative assistant. Now I was being invited to apply for a job where I would be in charge of an entire division of employees.

Fast forward: I got the job. The stunning revelation that was confirmation from God was calling my mother after the interview to share what I had learned about the history of the institution. It turned out that my grandmother and her sisters had attended that same institution decades earlier when it was a school for girl children of freed slaves, and they had even played basketball there! Not only did that give me chills, but it also gave me a sense of connectivity, responsibility, and affirmation! Like Alores C. Norris said in her business development book, *I May Not Be Perfect, But My Lipstick Is*, "Your ancestors did not manifest themselves into your soul to watch you become a convenient place for someone else's feet. My dear, you are a queen." (Norris, 2021). I knew it was time for me to step up instead of run.

Pursuing that job when I didn't feel qualified is something I would not have had the courage or skill set to do if I hadn't flipped my mindset and experienced some other successes. Doing scary things and not backing down from them is a skill that gets stronger and more refined the more you use it. Taking the leap toward that new job placed me in a new realm in my career and placed me on a trajectory that elevated my professional opportunities and allowed me to see myself in a whole new way—even to this day. I had begun to change from the inside out, and that new job was not only an external representation of my internal growth, but an opportunity to "leap into action."

Leaping While Exhausted

As the quality of my first marriage continued to decline over the years, I felt an increased sense of sadness and a constant desire to escape. I was honoring my duties as a wife, but I was not honoring myself at all. I had completely lost my identity, and I just felt utterly hopeless and lost.

I knew I had to do something drastic to save my life.

One day, it just hit me. I sat up straight in my bed, crust still in my eyes, with a feeling of clarity that seemed to permeate every fiber of my being. I wanted a divorce. Nothing about that decision was simple, but in that quiet moment early in the morning, it felt easy because there was such a spirit of certainty and a stillness that coupled with the decision.

After so many years of trying to make the marriage work and struggling with the concept of divorce, my sense of self-preservation was what ultimately prevailed. No matter who you are or what your situation is, that's never an easy conversation to have, but I had it. He responded with shock and anger, but I couldn't focus on that. I knew I had to find an attorney and have some other uncomfortable conversations with family and close friends. The decision to get a divorce was mine, and it came with several smaller, scary leaps into action, but I took each scary step—one at a time.

Some transformations are more happy than scary—those with fun, enlightening challenges along the way. But divorce is not one of them. Divorce is like death. I think anyone who values marriage but chooses divorce must be in a lot of pain. Somewhere inside, I knew a life of pain was not tied to what God had planned for me.

When you make and own a decision such as this, not everyone around you will agree with it and support it. That is why it's so important to flip your mindset *first,* so the subsequent steps will always be grounded in YOUR own decision to become the best version of yourself, not anyone else's idea of what you should be doing. Remember, when you take a step forward and upward, you are often also stepping away from your inner circle. In some situations, you'll be stepping away from people you love and care about deeply, people who have been around you your entire life. I was the first person in our family to get a divorce, but I am confident that doing so saved my life.

A Weighty Decision

My divorce leap strengthened me to overcome what had been a lifelong struggle—my weight. Not everyone grapples with weight management, and not everyone fights with it to the extent I had. However, if you have ever needed to lose even five pounds, you know the weight does not just magically fall off. You need to do something to get the results you want, and that has clearly been the case with my weight-loss journey.

As someone who had always carried extra weight for years, I had a lot of experience with attempting to lose weight. I was doing more wrong things than right things, but I just did not know any better.

Once again, I found myself in a situation where I had to leap into action to fight for my life. My first jump came in February 2016, when my doctor informed me that my cholesterol was high. My numbers had reached a level where my doctor was on the verge of prescribing medication to manage my cholesterol and reduce my risk for chronic heart disease. I was already taking medication for high blood pressure then, and didn't want to add anything else. Desperately wanting to avoid that scenario, I begged my doctor not to put me on medication, but instead give me a chance to reduce it on my own. She told me what to do.

I went home and threw away everything she advised me to remove from my diet: mayonnaise, butter, vegetable oil, Crisco, cheese, sour cream, coffee creamer, ice cream, full-fat yogurt, full-fat cottage cheese, ranch and onion dips, chips, bacon, whole eggs, deli meat, red meat, shrimp, creamed soups, Alfredo sauce, creamy salad dressings and more. When I returned to the doctor about six months later, my cholesterol levels had plummeted far below the high-risk range. She remarked that she had never before seen such a drastic change in any patient's cholesterol based solely on dietary changes. Then she started referring to me as her "star patient," which made me feel even more special. It boosted my confidence.

That accomplishment of moving the needle with my cholesterol, and the subsequent positive experience at my doctor's office, was incredibly empowering. I felt amazing. It also represented the first time I felt pleased and at ease at the doctor's office, compared to years of feeling fear, shame, worry, and disgust.

Although I felt better about myself, my challenge was that while my cholesterol had dropped, my weight had remained the same. Sadly, around this same time, my ex-husband died as a result of various medical problems, many of which were tied to the type of unhealthy lifestyle we had previously shared for 17 years.

My ex-husband's death was a wake-up call for me. The soberness of where my life was headed if I didn't make some changes forced me to acknowledge the harsh realities directly correlated with compulsive overeating and lack of exercise. I couldn't lie to myself anymore. I could not pretend I was somehow a different type of overweight person who was healthy and beating the odds—not when I saw my ex-husband lying in a casket at the age of 50, his children and family shocked and crying.

Drastic times called for drastic measures, so I took another scary leap and hired a personal trainer for the first time in my life. It was someone I had never met. Until then, I had only seen fitness trainers on weight-loss television shows. No one in my (caterpillar) life did things like hire personal trainers. It just wasn't a thing in our world.

Because it was something completely new for me, I was very nervous and lacked confidence. However, had heard about a woman who had lost 100 pounds with him. She is a real, live, breathing person, not someone I saw on television or in a magazine. Hearing about her major weight loss success let me know it could be done, and I believed this trainer could help me do it.

Hearing about my personal trainer was one thing, but I had to meet him and hire him. That was just the beginning because my next leap was to go to the gym and exercise. I am 5'2" tall and (at the time) weighed 304 pounds. I felt incredibly self-conscious about my appearance, was very physically inactive, and had no idea what to do at a gym other than walk on a treadmill. During my first workout with my trainer, I felt like I was going to die after the basic warm-up exercises. I was out of breath, sweating excessively, and my mobility was limited. I had to get over the fact that my body was bigger than most of the people around me, the excess fat on my arms, back, stomach, and thighs jiggled when I jumped around, and my body felt sore *all* the time.

Once I took that first step, I got over all those concerns. I realized no one at the gym was staring at me or making fun of me. In fact, everyone around me was super supportive, encouraging, and focused on their own fitness goals. People smiled, said, "hello," and gave me fist bumps. I could not have asked for a more welcoming environment. If I had never taken that first step of contacting the trainer, I would have never taken the other steps, and I would not have known that an amazing trainer, great gym, and loving fitness community could change my life forever. I have lost 140 pounds with that trainer, and he is still my trainer today. If I had not pushed through my fears, there is a good chance I might have died by now.

Just START!

Like the caterpillar, leaping into action by taking that first step onto the branch can be scary and requires balance. You might fall. In fact, you might fall multiple times, but if you keep trying, you will eventually conquer that first step.

For our caterpillar, balancing herself on the branch and getting used to climbing ever so slowly and steadily is critical. For humans, it is often about balancing the old version of ourselves with the new. It's about balancing and making room for new habits right on top of the obligations of work, motherhood, marriage, family, friendships, and everything else on our ever-growing, grown-up lists. It's about taking that first step without looking back and without worrying about what will happen if people see you fall. Falling does not mean failing.

Often, leaping into action requires extra support to maintain your balance. For me, that meant seeking not only the services of a personal trainer for weight loss, but also hiring a counselor and life coach. I needed to do my inside work to face my fears and stay the course for the long haul.

Accepting support is huge because no one does it alone. In fact, I never said you had to take your first step alone without any help. Nothing we have talked about so far requires solitude, and you will notice that everything I have mentioned so far has involved my seeking and accepting help... from my decision to continue my education to accepting a big new job, leaving a bad marriage, and overhauling my health and fitness.

You can do the same when taking your first leap into action in any area of your life—starting a business, starting a family, buying your dream house, etc. Whatever you want to achieve, your first action step will probably be a little scary (or terrifying). Remember, as you start the climb, you not only have the support of others along the way, but you are also building muscles while you climb— muscles such as discipline, time management, focus, trust, confidence, and persistence. These things, combined with your belief that you *can* do it and your determination to succeed, will allow you to hang on and continue the climb.

The irony is that even if you start your climb the right way, you may still fall, get yourself up, and try again. As you climb higher, you will be even closer to reaching your goal. That means you will be stronger and less likely to get bruised beyond repair if you *do* fall. You will have the strength to get back up. Not only will the branch (your support system) help you, but because you will be operating on a higher plane, you will start to see butterflies fluttering around, which will encourage and inspire you to want to be like them.

In other words, if you just START and trust the process, you will eventually be surrounded by like-minded individuals. You will find yourself among people who have already accomplished what you are working to achieve... but you don't get to experience any of this if you never START.

Just take the first, scary step, accept help along the way, and just... keep... going!

Wing Tips

My Incredible Journey: Leaping Into Action

- Of the goals I thought about at the end of the Chapter Three (Flip Your Mindset), which ones am I ready to pursue right now?
- What is the very first step I need to take to get started?
- What am I going to do to take that first step?
- When am I going to take that first step?
- How do I feel about getting started? Nervous? Terrified? Excited? Something else?
- Have I told (or do I plan to tell) anyone about my plans to pursue this goal? If no, why not? If yes, who?
- Who will be part of my support system?

- Do I need to hire a professional to help me?
- Will I need to adjust anything in my life to balance and accommodate my pursuit of this goal?
- What is the *second* step I need to take to progress toward this goal?

SECTION III

PHASE THREE:

Pupa ~ Chrysalis

When the caterpillar reaches its final size, it stops feeding.

The caterpillar wriggles and twists to gradually remove its old skin,

revealing a new protective skin called, "chrysalis."

Inside the chrysalis, the caterpillar changes

into a wormlike creature called, "pupa."

Unwelcome Visitor

Tired stopped by late this afternoon and said...

"I'm here to get you"

"I'm not ready to go," I said

But Tired didn't care

And started circling my desk, loudly clicking his pen repeatedly

Tired started leaning on my shoulders

Trying to push me into a slump

But I kept resisting, slapped away his hands

And said, "That's the best you got? Go on now"

Then Tired spun my chair around

Laughed sarcastically

And blew into my eyes until I had to rub them

"How did you even get in here?" I asked

"You need to leave now

I told you I'm not ready"

Right about that time, Lonely walked in

And said, "You'd might as well go on and leave

You know how Tired is. He's not going to give up

Besides, I've already got your dinner plate and glass of water

Waiting for you when you get home

Do you need me to pick up anything from the store?"

"Tonight's not a good night," I said to Lonely

But Lonely always lingered and ignored me

"I know what you need," he smiled

Then he leaned in close enough for me to feel his dark, scratchy

Beard on my ear as I cringed

And he whispered, "I know you better than you know yourself"

As he turned to leave, he said

"Oh, I told Guilt and Depression they could come over

To watch the game and hang out

They might stay for a few days

"But I…"

As the tail of his long, dark coat cleared the door

My cell phone rang

And I felt a teardrop run down my face

And drip to my collarbone

It was Love

But I didn't have the heart to answer the call

CHAPTER SIX

WHAT GOES AROUND COMES AROUND

I wonder how I would have felt about myself.

Within the first few months of the COVID-19 pandemic, like many people, I was seeking ways to keep my body moving to stay fit and remain connected with others. I was already working out virtually from home with my personal trainer every morning, but I wanted to do even more.

I found out that a trainer I knew was about to start a virtual hula hoop bootcamp. Familiar with her amazing hula hoop skills, I signed up right away. This woman made the hula hoop look so easy. I had seen her dance to music with one or more hula hoops twirling in perfect time to the music, no matter how fast or slow the song was. I honestly consider her to be the Michael Jackson of hula hooping, so I knew I was in for a treat.

Well, it was more a trick than a treat for me. It turns out that I was horrible at hula hooping. I didn't understand it; I had grown up hula hooping as a child. I recalled it as something I just did without thinking, not something for which I had to develop a special skill.

There were about eight of us women, all participating from our homes via Zoom. The idea of the bootcamp was that we would start by hula hooping for five minutes and then work our way up to continuously hula hooping for 30 minutes or more, which is an incredible source of cardio exercise.

Beginning on Day One (the five-minute day), I was the only person in the group who couldn't do it. I would place the hula hoop around my waist, and then simultaneously rotate my hips while giving the hoop a whirl to send it around. As I remembered from childhood, and could see with the other women, this large round circle was supposed to continue going around until I was ready for it to stop. Mine immediately fell to the ground each time—literally. It would twirl around my body about one and a half good times, just from the momentum of my original push, but that was it. I was burning calories, but my calories burned were the result of my bending down, repeatedly, to pick up the hula hoop from the ground.

The bootcamp instructor was trying her best to make it fun. She played music while we hooped, provided tips, and then, at some point, began to offer tips just for me. "Try putting your left foot forward a little more, Matteel, and see if that helps." Or "Rock your body in more of a forward and backward motion instead of rotating your hips." I wasn't having fun.

Why did all the other women make it look so easy? They were laughing and talking while their hula hoops appeared to twirl effortlessly around their waistlines. Whether we were on the first day, hooping for five minutes or on the seventh day, hooping for twenty minutes, the other ladies twirled effortlessly while I continued to spend my time bending up and down, picking the hula hoop up from the ground.

It was embarrassing. I did *not* want to be the one person in the group called out and needing special help because I just couldn't make it work the way it was supposed to. To add insult to injury, I asked my husband to give it a try one day, and he twirled it around his waist with ease, like a circus performer. He raised his hands in the air, smiled, laughed, and was clearly just having fun.

I am an adult. I wasn't required to take a hula hoop bootcamp class. I *chose* to do it. That means I could have quit at any time. My frustration level was high, and it was showing on my face, but I had committed to take part in the bootcamp and didn't want to give up. I really wanted to get it. It was just a hula hoop, after all. I was not going to allow this circular piece of plastic to win.

So, I dug in. I started asking for more help. I asked the instructor to watch what I was doing, and I asked questions. She provided more tips, and I asked more questions. Now, by this time, the other women had begun to practice some of the special little tricks the instructor had been teaching to help us burn more calories and make the entire experience more fun. I was still just trying to keep the hula hoop off the ground!

Well, it turns out that I was using the wrong hula hoop size. Who knew? I don't remember having to make such critical hula hoop decisions as a child, beyond whether I wanted the pink one or the striped one. There are so many things to know about hula hoops. They come in different diameters, weights, textures and widths. My instructor realized I needed the hula hoop that was just right for me (I told you she is an expert), so she dropped off a different hula hoop at a local gym, and I swung by and picked it up.

Guess what? I did it! I started hula hooping with the rest of the ladies. Applying all the other techniques I had been learning since the beginning of the bootcamp, I was twirling to the music, with the proper footwork and even attempted some of the tricks... and the hula hoop stayed UP! It was so much fun, and today hula hooping is one of my favorite cardio exercises. If you have the space, it's something you can do almost anywhere, even in your living room while watching TV. Do I now know more than I ever wanted to know about the *sport* of hula hoop? Yes, definitely... but mastering hula hooping was never the point. It was the goal, but it wasn't the lesson I was supposed to get.

I was supposed to practice my skill of not giving up. I set a goal, made a commitment, and stuck it out until the end. I didn't catch on until the last couple days of the bootcamp challenge, but the point is that I never gave up. To this day, I don't hate the hula hoop. In fact, I now own three!

I wonder how I would have felt about the sport of hula hoop today if I had dropped out of the bootcamp as soon as it got difficult—as soon as things weren't going as I had expected. More important, I wonder how I would have felt about myself. Even if I had stuck it out to the bitter end without mastering it, it would have still felt better than if I had just given up when it felt embarrassing, when it was frustrating, or when it wasn't fun anymore. I wonder how I would have felt if I had never stopped to ask for more help and accepted the proper tools.

By seeing it through to the end, I learned to adjust my attitude about the entire situation and see the whole thing as an opportunity rather than a failed mission. I was winning every time I stepped onto that back deck and logged into Zoom, and I was a winner every time I left the camera on because it would have been so easy, and so much more comfortable, to hide and not allow people to watch me while I struggled.

Can I twirl across the room like Michael Jackson, with one hula hoop around my waist and another around one of my arms? Nope. But I can remain in an upright position and keep the hula hoop off the ground. So, you know what? I'll take it. What goes around comes around, and for me that now includes the hula hoop, plus my strengthened ability to push through uncomfortable circumstances to reach my goals!

CHAPTER SEVEN

YIELD TO THE PAIN

The friends and family who were there for me when I was lonely and exhausted were like a branch for me.

Sometimes they were all I had to lean on to prevent me from giving up.

Dealing with being uncomfortable is a huge part of transforming from the inside out and reaching your goals. In fact, this is the step in the transformation process that made me an official expert in transformation. It was not the degrees on the wall, my experiences coaching others, nor anything else. It is this step—learning how to yield to the pain and not give up. If you don't make it through this step, then you simply do not reach your goal… period. This is the step that builds your muscles and makes you stronger, but this is also the place where most people give up. Even if you have to start over from the very beginning, you must still make it through this step to make it to the end in order to experience what it feels like to soar. This is the "never give up step." Any underdog movie that has ever had you cheering at the screen is because of this step.

If you are a person of faith, this is the step that will have you crying out to God to help you push through. This is the part you can't explain to others while you're in it because there's absolutely no way they will understand. They can't. It's your experience to have, but you CAN make it past this. This is why I said the first three steps are sooo important. I want you to get to the final two steps and enjoy all the goodness that happens there, but I need to teach you how to get through this point first. It will change your life forever.

In life, you must go through the pain to get to the good stuff... always, always, always. It's the order of life. All butterflies go through a life cycle comprising four distinct stages: *egg, larva, pupa,* and *adult.* This process of metamorphosis makes butterflies seem almost magical and enhances their overall interest and appeal. It is also a key component of their evolutionary success.

We commonly talk about caterpillars going into a cocoon stage while they're transforming. This is the pupal stage, which is often referred to as a "chrysalis." Because the caterpillar is basically naked (and therefore highly vulnerable) during this stage, a lot of work goes into concealing her appearance and location. While it may appear (to people looking in) that the chrysalis is simply hanging out, there is a TON of grueling work going on behind the scenes. It is an U-G-L-Y process. In fact, because of the remarkable way the tissues are being broken down and completely reorganized, one expert describes it as "a radical reconstruction from one form to another." (Daniels, 2018). Then the tissues begin to grow into new body parts. Once the internal transformation is complete, the new colors and patterns begin to show, signaling that a new adult butterfly is about to emerge.

If the conditions aren't just right with the disguises, chemicals, location, and even the way the larva attaches herself to the leaf (with silk), then she won't be able to hold on and persist. She might be eaten by a predator before she has a chance to finish developing. No matter what the cause, it means she will be just another caterpillar who began the process but never emerged, in a new form, to experience her dream of living life as a butterfly.

Another fascinating part of this stage of the process is that you and I cannot help her. That's right. She must do the work by herself and make her way out of the cocoon and back onto the branch to finish the journey to the top and then fly. If we see her struggling, we may continue to offer support. However, we must resist the temptation to get in there and rescue her. She must do her own work, and if we help her out of the cocoon, she will still surface as a butterfly, and she will still make it to the top of the branch. However, she will never be able to fly on her own. How sad would that be—to make it that far and still not have the full experience of living life as a butterfly?

Exhausted and Overwhelmed

My higher education journey gave me the full experience of ascending and transforming—good and bad. Fortunately, I was able to earn my bachelor's degree by taking college classes in the evening at a satellite location right on the campus where I worked. I couldn't ask for anything more convenient than that. I still had to put in the work though, because it was an intensive program from a reputable institution. We met in person for several hours, three evenings per week, and completed one class every four or five weeks, and then immediately moved on to the next one. The program was rigorous. I was working full time, getting by in an unfulfilling marriage, and completing college classes one month at a time.

Being in a hyper-focused mode required me to decline social engagements so I could focus on my homework. I used lunch breaks and time on the weekends to do what I needed to do to earn my degree. This type of schedule, constant pressure, and minimal down time left me feeling exhausted and lonely most of the time. When I started working on my master's degree, I was still married to my first husband, and we were living in a small town, an hour away from where I had to attend classes. To get there, I had to travel at night on a heavily wooded, two-lane, back road through tiny, rural towns populated mostly with people who didn't look like me, and with limited cell phone reception. Once I arrived on campus, I always faced the arduous task of continuously circling parking lots that looked like shopping mall parking lots during the Christmas holidays. You know the scene, where you see someone walking toward a vehicle and pray that they're leaving so you can grab their spot. I also had to figure out how and when to eat dinner. These things might sound mundane and normal. However, for me, all these things added little pockets of stress and were isolating. I just had to keep going, keep pushing, focus on the positive, and figure it out so I could reach my goal.

At times, I also had to return to campus on weekends to access the library or a special computer lab or meet with classmates to work on group projects. I also used a lot of my vacation time because I needed to leave work early to make it to class on time, or I needed extra time off to complete a paper or project. In other words, there was really no time for fun or enjoyment. Even my vacations consisted of work for school, and everything throughout the week and on the weekends was work and school, work and school... rinse and repeat.

Later, when my parents traveled that route with me to attend my commencement ceremony, they were horrified when they realized the route their daughter had been driving alone at night to earn a degree. Just like the butterfly larva goes to great lengths to complete her work under the cover of darkness and in less-than-ideal conditions, I did what I had to do.

There were times when I was exhausted and turned the car radio louder just to stay awake; and was hungry because I didn't have time to eat anything between the time I left work and walked into the classroom. Sometimes, in moments of low self-esteem, I compared myself to my classmates and felt afraid I wasn't good enough to perform well in the classes. Other times, I felt afraid because I didn't have time to stop for gas and feared I might run out of gas alone on one of those dark, quiet, back country roads. Although I felt scared, I knew God was with me every step of the way, so I never gave up. It would have been quite easy to quit, but I didn't—and it paid off. That was the road (literally and figuratively) to earning my master's degree. Commitment trumped convenience!

After earning my master's degree, I started working on my PhD. By that time, I was also adapting to my new vice president's position in a new city, buying a house, and navigating divorce. I was still exhausted and isolated from my family, who were now four hours away, and I was being stretched far beyond my comfort zone in so many ways. There were times when I wanted to give up. I recall tearfully announcing to my friend Janice that I was going to quit, give up, and walk away because I just couldn't do it anymore.

Like a mama bear, Janice fiercely blocked all that self-deprecating talk and protected me from my self-inflicted negativity. She knew the details about everything I had on my plate, but she would not allow me to throw in the towel. This is an example of why it is so important to surround yourself with people who genuinely care about you, understand your goal, and are willing to support you. In this case, Janice was there to support me emotionally and hold me accountable. By the way, fast forward... I was able to give it back to my friend Janice several years later when she began to grow weary during her own doctoral journey. I am proud to say that she is now DOCTOR Janice T. Lyle! You go, girl! I'm proud of you.

When that caterpillar changes her mindset and then leaps into action by stepping onto the branch, she has begun her journey in a supportive environment. That support will remain in place and help her hold on even when it's painful, and a lot is going on behind the scenes. The friends and family who were there for me when I was lonely and exhausted were like a branch for me. Sometimes they were all I had to lean on to prevent me from giving up. No one could do the work for me, but they offered me words of encouragement. They made me laugh. They prayed for me. They gave me food so I wouldn't worry about cooking, and they gave me stern words when I needed them. I had one classmate, Willette, now a dear friend, who would write with me on the weekends. She lived more than an hour away but needed a quiet place to write; and we both needed the accountability. So, we isolated ourselves for the weekend and wrote our hearts out—only stopping to leave the house for dinner at a nice restaurant each evening.

Like the caterpillar on her way to becoming a butterfly, not only did I *not* have to make the journey alone... I *could not* have made the journey alone.

Sometimes the support had to come from deep down. For example, I needed to say "no" to invitations to participate in fun activities like going to a movie with a friend, going shopping or dining out with friends. I lost some friendships with people who just couldn't fully understand and appreciate my circumstances, and that was okay. I had neither the time nor the energy to try to explain. Well, let me restate that—I usually *did* try to explain, but sometimes they just couldn't understand. Some of those friendships have been restored and others have not, but I continue to trust in God that everything happens the way it is supposed to and that everything has its season.

I went on to earn that terminal degree, and now this first-generation college graduate is Dr. Matteel D. Knowles. I am so glad I held on. Thank you, God! Thank you!

Lonely Near the Top

One thing good mentors will tell you is that as you ascend up the ladder to higher positions, things get lonelier. However, I had no idea how painful that type of isolation could be or how hard it would be to hold on at times. You see, sometimes there's a different, scrappier type of competition at the top. As a first-generation college graduate turned executive-level leader, I had no idea what it would be like at the top of the organizational chart.

In pretty much every organization, executives are under tremendous pressure for various reasons and are all usually vying for the same limited resources. It's a lot like the journey to becoming a butterfly. To survive long enough to experience the full transformation, the caterpillar usually has to use clever disguises to fool her would-be predators. She learns how to hide out, take on unusual allies (like ants), and develop hard shells to survive the vulnerable chrysalis (cocoon) stage before emerging as an adult butterfly.

Similarly, the journey to an executive-level position is much more challenging than what other people may see looking in from the outside. Like the butterfly in the cocoon, the only thing those on the outside see are the beautiful colors beginning to form. However, in executive roles, it is rarely as beautiful on the inside as it appears on the exterior. It is a constant balancing act. Time rarely seems to be on your side. The hours at work get longer and the lines of demarcation between home, work, fun, and rest but become increasingly blurry—or disappear altogether if you're not careful.

When I first began to grow into new roles, the people around me were not always happy for me. For example, it was incredibly awkward when people I worked with as peers suddenly became my subordinates on the organizational chart, and I had to guide, support, and even discipline them at times.

I remember a time when my boss pulled everyone in the office together for a quick, stand-up meeting where she announced that I would be the new director. There were about eight of us standing in a tight semi-circle behind a set of cubicles. I stood next to the manager, facing the others, as she shared the news with them. I don't recall what people said, but I clearly remember the reaction was unusually quiet, and I observed side glances and sentiments left unspoken in that moment. It was simple. They were not happy for me. In an instant, it had changed everything. However, going through things like that and enduring the type of pain and isolation that accompanied complicated transitions made me stronger.

Like the caterpillar forming into a butterfly in that chrysalis stage, over time, I learned to seek emotionally safe relationships through my mentors and friendships and worry less about predators. By embracing the wisdom of others and accepting support, those relationships allowed me to hold on and focus on the reasons why God had placed me in certain situations at particular times to make me stronger and wiser.

Real transformation requires core strength, and the workplace usually comes with what often feels like endless character-building opportunities. You have to learn how to navigate situations with people from different backgrounds, mindsets, motivations, and even different reasons for being there in the first place. You will probably have many occasions to lean into some type of challenge and try to get the lesson from it. Sometimes there will be a lot going on behind the scenes, and the lessons will be painful, but those situations will always present opportunities for personal growth.

Like the caterpillar soon to emerge as a butterfly, yielding to the pain is just part of the natural process of making a radical transformation from one form to another. You just need to let the process be the process and develop the skills you need to persist.

Dark and Lonely

While a deep sense of loneliness can occur while moving up the ladder in the workplace, it can also occur in other types of transformations. Some of the most profound experiences of loneliness often surface in the midst of personal relationships that are transforming in some way.

As with every type of major transformation, you are going to go through darkness before you get to the light. What added to the dark period for me was the divorce process started while my ex-husband and I still resided in the same house. I used a ton of strategy and energy to avoid interacting with him. One day, a friend who was in town for business stopped by the house to pick me up so we could catch up over dinner. It was her first time being around me and my husband since I had initiated the divorce. I don't recall the circumstances that triggered it, but he came downstairs and exploded into an angry outburst in front of her. My nerves were already on edge because of the tense household situation and what he might do. I felt so mortified that I was physically shaking. My friend was also visibly shaken and speechless. That was the first time someone from outside the house had been exposed to the hidden tension that existed in our world behind the closed doors. We canceled dinner, and I apologized profusely. Her concerned eyes met mine as she turned to leave the house. I shut the door behind her and just stood there.

I knew my friend was worried and felt sorry for me. I felt sorry for myself too, but I didn't have the luxury of time to wallow in that emotion. I had work to do, so I had to yield to the painful realities of temporarily living in the same house with someone who was no longer active in a relationship with me. He was angry. I was exhausted, and I never had a safe, quiet place to relax and rejuvenate... but, through God's grace, I remained steadfast and determined to persist with my goal of dissolving the marriage.

Every day, I went to work where there was also a lot of stress, then to school in the evenings... more stress... and then back home to an atmosphere thick with negative energy... stress, stress, stress. I existed like this for months. No one could have lived in that situation for me. I had to go through it by myself, on my own, even though it was painful. I know I only survived the pain of that time through the grace of God and the people with whom He surrounded me for wisdom, encouragement, and support.

Divorce also gutted me financially. As the plaintiff seeking the divorce, I was immediately required to pay $1,000 per month in spousal support for a year once my husband left the house. That financial commitment was followed by the $750 per month alimony I had to pay to him for five years—all while maintaining a lifestyle that had been built for two incomes.

Within the first couple of years following our divorce, my car (which was paid off) completely broke down beyond repair. Both the engine and transmission needed to be replaced, so I had no choice but purchase a new car. As painful as that realization was, there is a silver lining to this story, and it is something that truly confirmed God's presence and support in my life.

Right before my car died, I had refinanced the mortgage on the house and the monthly mortgage payment dropped by $380. When I purchased my new car, the monthly payment for that was $380.01. Won't He do it? It was moments like that when I was reminded that I was not alone, and it could only have been God. Like the caterpillar changing into a butterfly in that cocoon, I still had a branch, something to hold onto. I still had support in God. I wasn't completely alone, and I didn't have to figure it out on my own. So, I held onto hope for something better to come, despite the darkness and the pain of my cocoon stage.

Still, I created a lot of credit card debt trying to hold it all together. There were times when I had to use credit cards to pay for basics like groceries and toothpaste. For nine years, I attempted to maintain the former marital home, but by then I had relocated four hours away. I was taking care of a new house I had purchased, while still trying to handle the mortgage and repair costs for our former home, and that mortgage was $2,000 per month plus an exorbitant HOA fee. All of that proved to be more than I could handle, so I surrendered. As a result, the former marital home went into foreclosure and my healthy 770 credit score immediately plummeted to 645. Thankfully, by the grace of God, the foreclosure process did not result in any additional debt. My credit cards are now all paid off, and my credit score is almost back to where it was.

I realize I could have given up. I took a hit... and then a punch... and a slap... and even got burned a few times... but you know what? I hung in there. It might sound odd to some, but yielding to the pain of divorce and allowing the process to be the process provided me with some of the most profound lessons of my life.

Ironically, although I feel like I lost myself during my first marriage, I really got to know myself better during the divorce—some things I liked and some I didn't. Going through all of that broke me, humbled me, and taught me that I CAN get to the other side of horrible experiences in life if I hold on, yield to the pain, accept it as a natural part of the transformation process, and trust God's support. My goal was to survive divorce as the best version of myself—healthy and whole, and I can honestly say I did that.

The Pain of Public Failure

Holding on and getting to the other side of challenging transformations definitely makes you stronger, and that determination to succeed has been a common thread throughout my weight-loss journey. When you lose massive amounts of weight like I have (and you do it naturally), it doesn't come without sacrifice, challenges, and uncertainty. Even while writing this book, I was living the "yield to the pain" part of weight loss in a major way.

In 2009, I weighed 352 pounds. By the time I made it to my personal trainer in 2016, I was down to 304 pounds. Working with him, I made it as low as 164 pounds. My ultimate goal for the scale is 142 pounds.

Those are the numbers, the statistics, the *before* and *after*, but people rarely understand what happens in between to get there.

Getting serious about losing weight to get healthy required all the things we have discussed in the first two chapters, but man, oh man, have I learned how to hold on? I once read a quote that I love: "The key to success is figuring out how not to quit." Like the caterpillar in the process of doing her work to transform into a butterfly, when you are on a weight-loss journey, you have to figure out how to keep going and try not fall.

Just like the dynamic and transitional chrysalis stage for the developing butterfly, weight loss does not happen overnight. Weight loss isn't nice, neat, consistent, predictable, or pretty. Weight loss is not your friend, and it is not your enemy. It's fickle and *sometimey*. What you do for a few months that works steadily and effortlessly can suddenly turn on you and just stop working. Those in the process of losing massive amounts of weight are accustomed to this, and often refer to those challenging times as "plateaus." Without proper support, those can be very painful and discouraging mileposts along a weight-loss journey, and this is where many people who are trying to lose weight give up and fall.

As with the butterfly transformation, when you get to the dark, challenging parts, you should accept the support, but do your own work without losing sight of your goal. That's a big part of why it's helpful to work with a reputable professional like a certified personal trainer, your primary physician, or a nutritionist. These professionals will know how to help you, but you still must do your part by trusting the process and never giving up. YOU have to put in the work and there's no way around it.

Throughout my weight-loss journey, my strategy has been to do exactly what my trainer told me to do. I ate food for breakfast that I didn't necessarily enjoy (like plain egg whites with spinach and plain oatmeal). I worked out at the gym, and sometimes at home, to achieve not only weight loss but the changes I desired in my physical appearance. Depending on where I was along the journey, there have been times when I have gotten up at 4:00 a.m., driven 30 minutes from home to the gym, and worked out with my trainer. I then drove back home, showered, dressed, drove to work, worked all day, and then drove back to the gym, did an hour of cardio, and then drove 30 minutes back home.

Somewhere in there, I had to eat meals I had prepped over the weekend, and consistently consume about a gallon of water each day, as I have now done for several years.

Over the past few years, I have continued to follow some sort of meal plan and work out five or six times each week. I still prep meals, but now I do it for myself and my husband, and I still go to the gym several days each week. It's what I need to do to reach my goals, and it's what I will need to do for the rest of my life to maintain the quality of life I desire and deserve. I have a scale goal, a look I want for my body, and I also have a weightlifting goal, because I eventually plan to participate in powerlifting competitions. Most importantly, I have mindset goals that align with all these things.

About a year and a half ago, I got to the point where I was 22 pounds away from my ultimate goal weight. I had even met with two surgeons to explore my options for surgery to remove loose skin from certain areas of my body. It was very exciting to be so close to my goal. Then suddenly, everything I was doing, and even the new things my trainer told me to do to break what I thought was a plateau, just stopped working. Not only did those things stop working, but I actually began gaining weight—a pound or two per week at first and eventually three to four pounds every single week. I could not make it stop.

It turned out that a previously diagnosed issue with my thyroid had flared up, resulting in significant weight gain—about 90 pounds. It was demoralizing, embarrassing, frustrating, and depressing. That is honestly how I felt. I had to purchase larger clothing in sizes that had previously become too large for me (those sizes I had already donated to others). I even had to buy a new coat—twice. To get so close to my goal and then experience such a major public setback right before the finish line was gut-wrenching. I was battle weary.

The difference is—I had become a new woman. I was no longer a caterpillar at the bottom of the branch. Through that failure and the work it took to hold on and not give up, I had grown stronger. Because I had flipped my mindset when I started my weight-loss journey, and because I had experienced so much success with all my transformations, I had figured out how to *not* quit.

Despite all the negative emotions like embarrassment, frustration, exhaustion, anger, imposter-syndrome, and fear associated with unexpected weight gain, I never gave up or stopped imagining myself achieving my goal.

I understand the many important life lessons in this experience, so I no longer view it as a failure. The word "FAIL" can be used as an acronym that stands for "FOR ALL I LEARNED."

Although mentally exhausted from being on a multi-year weight-loss journey, I choose to embrace the weight-gain phase as something I was supposed to go through for the purpose of learning and personal growth. As with so many other things in my life, I know there's going to come a time when I will have a "Wow, if I hadn't gone through that, I would not be where I am today" moment. I know it will all make sense later because it always does. God truly *does* work in mysterious ways.

Yes, I had gained back 90 pounds of the weight I had lost. Yes, I have to re-lose the weight I had already lost. Yes, I must do it in front of people who were previously cheering me on.

Sometimes, I could see that people wanted to ask what happened. Sometimes, I shared it with them. Other times, I didn't feel like it. It was *my* business, *my* pain, *my* work. I had developed enough confidence to understand that I didn't owe an explanation to anyone. However, I also know there is incredible value in being transparent and sharing about any painful challenges I have experienced during this, and other, transformations. Doing so presents an opportunity to not only be transparent and show that I am human, but it gives me an opportunity to demonstrate how to hold on and not give up, so I may teach and inspire others. It also helps others who are going through, or have gone through, the same thing.

I am not the first person in this situation, and I won't be the last, but I love that I never give up. I just hold onto my support system, trust the branch will be there, and I just don't give up. I keep going. I keep persisting toward my weight-loss goal, and I can't wait to have that butterfly experience with the people who love and support me right there by my side celebrating with me!

Everything Always Works Out!

I considered naming this part of the transformation process, "GRIT!" because at the end of the day, that is what's required to endure the pain of transformation and never, ever, ever give up. When fully grown, the butterfly larva seeks a secure location and attaches herself to a branch for support. In this situation, she is largely defenseless and just has to hold on, adapt to her new surroundings, and focus on the rigorous work that lies ahead for her in order to transform.

That's what is required when we want to transform during the hard parts. We have to hold on, even though everything inside us is telling us to give up. We cannot listen to or trust those voices. Our resolve may feel as fragile as silk adhered to a leaf, but we can never give up. That's what it means to yield to the pain. It's necessary to let the process flow and allow each experience to occur, with the full confidence that everything will work out fine in the end.

We are all going to face situations in life, especially when pursuing a major transformation, but those who make it through have learned how to hold on, accept support, and do their work despite the pain. They have grown to understand they don't get to skip doing their own work, they must go through it—all of it. Like the caterpillar in the cocoon, the branch will always be present. That's the support system, but it is the chrysalis that must hold on, do the work and push through to transform into a completely new creature. With the caterpillar becoming a butterfly, that literally must come from inside (from the interior), and it is the same with us as humans.

The world is filled with people who quit when the going gets tough. There are already enough of them. We need more people who are committed to holding on, even when doing so feels unbearably painful. My husband, a personal trainer, always tells his clients to "get comfortable with being uncomfortable."

Any time you are becoming something you have never been before, you're likely to experience something that will disrupt your progress and cause you to slide a little, but you don't have to fall back to where you started. If you fall, if you slip a little, brush yourself off, get the lesson, and keep it moving—stronger, wiser, and more determined than ever.

You must approach transformation journeys in your life by deciding from the beginning that you are willing to go through the pain until you get to the other side and reach your goal. Grounded with a proper mindset, it will be your conviction, your commitment, and your consistency that will carry you through. For those who hold on, everything always works out. One way or another, everything… always… works… out!

Wing Tips

My Incredible Journey:
Yielding to the Pain

- What are some things I already know that will probably make my pursuit of this goal challenging?

- How am I going to stay on track when those things happen?

- What am I going to do when unexpected things happen along the way that threaten my progress?

- When things get tough, what am I going to remind myself about? Why did I start working on this goal in the first place?

- Who will be part of my support system once I really get going? Will they be the same people who were with me when I started?

- What's going to help me push through when I want to quit.

SECTION IV

PHASE FOUR:

Adult Butterfly

When adulthood arrives, the pupa changes

into a butterfly and leaves the chrysalis.

The butterfly pumps blood into its wrinkled wings

and expands them to full size before flying away.

Angel

And the angel came down and enveloped her

Wrapped her arms softly around her

Like a cocoon

The sound of her wings as she drew near

Had been louder than what she could have ever imagined

Drowning almost

But not scary

Rhythmic and beautiful

And mystical and quiet and loud all at the same time

She held her close and she breathed

They breathed together

And smiled

And laughed a nervous laugh

Until she shuddered and then relaxed

And the angel told her to believe in herself
She told her she was special
And she told her she was kind
And she squeezed her a little tighter
And told her everything would be just fine

And the woman cried

The woman fell back with her arms spread wide
And she cried
And she wailed
And she moaned
And she thrashed

And all the while the angel held her

She cried until she was exhausted
And like a child
She fell asleep in the angel's arms

And then she began to dream

CHAPTER EIGHT

Round Up!

In spite of the mess, I felt so proud of myself.

Anyone who works with me knows that I can't stand having things half-done. I'm that person who will redo a report five times if that's what it takes to get it just right. I think that's one of the reasons why I vibe so well with my personal trainer. From the beginning, he taught me to do things like run *all the way* to the end and back when I'm running sprints—not just almost to the end. You can finish something but still not "finish finish." If you hear that little voice in your head saying, "I'll just..." then you are probably about to not "finish finish." I get it. I'm talking a good game here but I'm totally that person who won't measure before I hang a picture on the wall, and won't create hospital corners when making the bed, but it's very important to practice completion until it becomes a habit because it spills over into so many other things.

For example, I recently decided I was going to get up early one morning and finally deal with the weeds in the beds in front of the house. Now, let me be clear. I am neither a yard person nor a master gardener. I am not one of those people who, when asked what they did over the weekend, says (with a big smile on their face) that they worked in the yard, and then they are excited to describe what they did. The fact is that I love having a beautiful yard, but I don't want to put in the work. I would rather pay someone else to do it.

But here's the thing… in life, we cannot just hand over our issues for someone else to handle them. Sometimes you have to get a little dirty yourself and round up (weed-killing pun intended) the courage and commitment to see things through to make sure they're the way you know they need to be.

Now, we have a yard guy but he's basically someone who keeps the yard mowed, treats the grass from time to time, and lays down new mulch for us at the right time during the season. He will do whatever we ask him to do, but he's not a full-time landscaper. Plus, he doesn't live with us. He is not at our house 24/7, making sure that every little thing is good with our yard every day. He helps us, but at the end of the day, our yard is our responsibility, so we ought to have some skin in the game to keep it nice.

So that brings me back to that morning and the weeds out front. I put on my Crocs, grabbed my yard work gloves, and a large black trash bag. Timing is important, so I made sure I was outside while the ground was still moist, and it wasn't too hot.

I started along the edge of one of the beds. I bent down and pulled one of the weeds. Only the green part came out and I knew that, when pulling weeds, I needed to get all of it. I needed to pull it from the roots... so I moved my hand a little deeper and pulled a little harder. It came right out of the ground with ease.

I continued this throughout the two beds in front of the house. Some weeds were more mature than others, so the roots were a little more developed. For those, I had to use two hands to pull them out from the roots. There were more weeds out there than I realized, and I was surprised at how deep and how wide some of the roots ran. It surely pays to pull the weeds before they spread like that. In fact, there were some weeds that were spread out so wide on top of the mulch that I had mistaken them for several weeds, but that wasn't the case. It was just one large weed we had allowed to grow and fester for so long that it had spread out wide like a stayed-a-little-too-long houseguest on your sofa with his feet on your coffee table. Those weeds had to go.

What was interesting about those particular weeds is that they looked overwhelming from the top, but once I got my hands around them and grasped, they also came out of the ground with ease. That area of the bed immediately looked so much better.

Something else I realized was that there were a lot of little weeds starting to grow. I hadn't even noticed them until I got in close to do the work of pulling weeds. I made sure to get those as well because I had learned (from the bigger weeds) what would happen if I didn't deal with those as soon as I saw the problem brewing.

As I continued to do the work, I realized I wasn't hating it. It was not as difficult or as miserable as I had made it out to be in my mind. In fact, a neighbor walked by with her dog, and I gave her one of those very friendly, vibrant, "Good morning!" greetings. Was I actually *enjoying* this? Was I *enjoying* pulling weeds?

I realized what I was enjoying was the inner sense of pride I was getting from dealing with a problem that had been buried; a problem I had been walking by every day, ignoring and pretending it wasn't there. I could literally see the problem, and I had the tools I needed to get the job done, but I had just kept walking and watching the problem grow a little more each week.

My ego was enjoying being seen as the kind of person who handles things. We live in a nice subdivision, and it felt better to be seen as the type of homeowner who has a sense of pride of ownership, cares about how things look, cares about our community, and cares about doing her part to keep things nice. I enjoyed giving off the kind of energy to the world that lets people know that it's not just about me. It's about all of us. Just like in other areas of our lives, when we work on our own stuff, it also affects others around us.

So, I kept working my way through the beds out front until I had finished pulling all the weeds. It looked sooooo much better. I did not realize how bad it had gotten. Wow! I had gotten quite comfortable and adjusted to things being mediocre. I also knew I needed to pull a couple of weeds in the backyard. We have a tree back there with mulch and I had been noticing (and ignoring) those weeds as well.

What I didn't realize was that there were weeds along the side of the house, too. I don't go to that side of the house very often. It's where the HVAC unit is located and there were weeds growing around that as well. Although this was not a part of my original plan, I also took the time to pull those out from the roots. Once

I knew better, I had to do better. That area immediately looked better. I saw another type of low-growing weed with flowers that I didn't have the proper tools to address. I'll figure out what to do about those so I can go back and complete the job.

I finally made it to the backyard and pulled the two weeds that were in the bed around the tree. When I turned around to head back to the front of the house, I noticed weeds along the back of the house. Because I had never gone to deal with the weeds around the tree, I never had the vantage point of seeing the back of the house from that angle; but I also had another decision to make.

At that moment, I had to decide whether I was going to complete this job thoroughly or just head back around to the front. It occurred to me that no one sees the weeds in the back of the house except me. The neighbors walking their dogs wouldn't see them, and I wouldn't even have to see them. I could just ignore the problem and pretend it wasn't there, but this job was about completion. Just because others can't see the problem doesn't mean the problem doesn't exist, and it doesn't mean it still won't get out of hand. It was mine to deal with, so I bent down and pulled those weeds from their roots as well. I finished the job.

Sometimes you've got to get a little dirty to complete the work. By the time I finished pulling everything, my Crocs were wet with little pieces of grass stuck to them, and I had a large trash bag filled with weeds. In spite of the mess, I felt so proud of myself. I had a wonderful sense of accomplishment after completing something I didn't actually want to do in the first place, but knew I needed to get it done.

I know I won't ignore the weeds anymore. In the future, I know I will address the problem head on as soon as I see it coming to the surface. I know it will be easier to deal with it when it's still small, and I also know that because I pulled those weeds from the roots and didn't just deal with them on the surface level, those same weeds are never coming back. I did the work. I dealt with them, so they are gone forever.

Will there ever be weeds again in the beds around our house? Absolutely. Others will try to get in and take over, but I will recognize them, and I will know how to deal with them in a way that is so thorough that I won't have to deal with that same problem repeatedly. I have completely transformed our surroundings, and I prefer this look, so I'm never going to allow it to get the way it was before!

CHAPTER NINE

COMPLETE YOUR PROCESS

True completion means you use all the discipline muscles
and other skills developed during the climb
to courageously navigate the world in a whole new way.

The Butterfly

I don't know if you noticed, but the acronym for the first three steps in my transformation model (**F**lip Your Mindset, **L**eap into Action, and **Y**ield to the Pain) spells the word "FLY." This, of course, is what the caterpillar gets to do once she completes her transformation and becomes a full-fledged butterfly.

After the caterpillar has dug in and finished her work in the cocoon, she surfaces as a butterfly—a completely new being inside and out. She's still on the branch that provided support along the way, but she's not quite ready to fly on her own. She still needs just a little extra support. Although she is tired, she is completely different inside and out, and is on the other side of the hardest parts of her transformation. In other words... she made it!

In nature, this is the point at which "the adult butterfly will hang from the old chrysalis... and begin to pump hemolymph (its version of blood) into the veins of its wings." (Daniels, 2018). This action causes them to expand rapidly. Although this is what she had always hoped for, she must now get used to navigating the world with wings!

When you see photos depicting the outcome of the process that a caterpillar goes through in nature, the images show a stunningly beautiful adult butterfly. For humans, though, this is one of the points at which many of us give up and never fly—assuming the process is over. But... that's not *really* completion. We do *not* come that far just to—*come* that far, sit there and look pretty.

True completion means you use all the discipline muscles and other skills developed during the climb to navigate the world courageously, in a whole new way. That is why it's so good that the supportive branch is still there. Can you imagine how shocking it would be to her system if the caterpillar went into the cocoon one way and then came out as a butterfly with nothing to hold on to at first and no blood running through her wings to sustain her? It would be like a deaf person being able to hear for the first time or a blind person being able to see for the first time. Experiencing the world in a new way would be a blessing, but at the same time totally overwhelming. It's normal to expect a period of adjustment in nature, and it is the same with humans.

A New Identity

When I completed the requirements to earn my PhD, it felt like I was in the middle of a whirlwind, as though I had blinked and become a new person. It was an incredibly surreal feeling, but fortunately, a friend with a PhD had warned me it would be like that. She explained, "One day you go to bed and the next day you wake up as *Dr.*" I needed a little time to adjust to the change because I had not only earned a new degree—I had also assumed a new professional identity.

In the higher education sector, the doctoral degree is highly desired and respected. Some people started treating me differently at work—almost deferring to me. They would say things like, "I don't feel right just calling you Matteel." That was quite weird and uncomfortable at first, because I had previously lived most of my life as a caterpillar. I had always been down low and fearful of being crushed. Although the self-esteem I gained during the transformation journey had prepared me to feel more comfortable with appropriate attention, it was still new.

Over time, I realized people were sincerely proud of me, especially those within my African American community. African Americans typically earn about seven percent of all doctoral degrees awarded to American citizens each year, according to The Journal of Blacks in Higher Education (March 2021), and I was one of them. In comparison, only about eight out of 400 butterfly eggs live to become adult butterflies.

I had become a butterfly, so the reaction to my accomplishment made sense—especially from a community of African American people who are historically so underrepresented in higher education. Their feedback was a sign of respect I needed to learn to appreciate and embrace with comfort.

I also had to get used to the idea that people listened differently to what I had to say. My ideas, points of view, and opinions influence others because I earned a PhD. The awareness that what I had to say could inspire others lit a fire inside me that is still with me to this day, because I realized I *do* have something to say. I have a voice that can uplift, motivate, and positively impact others, whether it's in the boardroom, on the stage as a keynote speaker, or on the phone with a friend. That voice did not come as a result of earning a PhD. However, the process of earning it and the satisfaction that came from completing it gave me the courage to recognize my value and stop hiding the gifts and talents God gave me.

Upon the suggestion of a friend, I started adding "PhD" to things like my personal checks, my email signature block, etc. I had fun with it, but what it really did was formally mark the completion of that journey. Like the new, adult butterfly—who remains on the branch for a few hours after emerging from the cocoon to spend a little time pumping blood into her wings to expand them before flying—I was preparing myself to soar in my new identity as Dr. Matteel!

Invigorated!

While the caterpillar completes her journey by transforming into a butterfly getting ready to fly, I think of my career advancements as opportunities for continuous growth and exploration. I view each completion as the beginning of a new climb, a new caterpillar moment, a new opportunity to apply my transformation skills to a new goal and soar at new heights. For example, once I advanced from working as an administrative professional who supported executives to then becoming a mid-level manager leading a team, I had completed that journey. However, I still needed to apply my transformation skills to the next goal of serving as an executive-level leader.

The type of momentum that comes from completing one thing and then applying my new knowledge and skills to the next thing is incredibly invigorating and rewarding. Each time, it leaves me feeling like I can take on the world and accomplish whatever I want, because the basic steps are the same, and I know how to navigate them and reach my goal.

<u>The Relationship is Complete</u>

I once saw a quote that read, "Don't say the relationship is over, say it's complete. Some aren't meant to last forever." Just like the caterpillar's life must naturally come to an end to make room for her new existence as a butterfly, the completion step in some relationships is a critical part of personal transformation for real growth to occur.

This type of natural ending of one thing and the beginning of another can relate to friendships, family connections, and romantic love interests. In my life, I have definitely had relationships that were for a particular season in my life—usually so I could get a lesson or a blessing, or be a lesson or a blessing for someone else. Most times, it made sense later, but one thing all those relationships had in common was that they came to a clear and distinct end... they ran their course... they completed.

As I have experienced different types of transformation over the years (and have grown from those experiences), part of what I learned was the value and the naturalness of letting go. I have let go of friendships that started off great and served me in the beginning, but were no longer healthy for me.

Even in my family, over time, I learned to establish boundaries with certain family members. In doing so, the relationship dynamics also changed, but that was okay. In the workplace, I have intentionally disassociated with people who no longer added value to my experience there because they were negative, gossipy, and focused on what had gone wrong or what might go wrong.

In each of those situations, something was there for me in the beginning and then at some point my mindset changed, and I evolved into a different type of person with a new identity and a new set of interpersonal skills and life goals. I grew to understand that not everyone was meant to stay with me throughout my entire journey.

How I navigated the process of completing my first marriage was just as important as my decision in the beginning to end it. I had to get the lessons around characteristics such as patience, humility, faith, trust, vulnerability and more. To expand my wings, I first had to become reacquainted with my authentic self. I did that by forming new relationships, spending time alone, writing creatively, and working with a professional counselor.

I had to trust God fully and completely, with a deep knowing that everything would be okay, no matter what. I had to be patient and keep my mind and spirit as calm as possible as the relationship ended. I chose to be kind to my ex-husband and his family, and to be kind and gentle with myself. I'm so glad I did because it greatly helped with my healing process as I moved forward with my new life.

Like the newly formed butterfly, I was preparing to fly, *not* remain stagnant on the branch. I was intentional about releasing bitterness and resentment that did not serve my growth. I came out on the other side whole, healed, restored, and ready to charge into the next phase of my life. Not all transformations are about happy situations, but the value of seeing the process through to the end is the same.

Gradually Emerging

Completion still lies ahead for me when it comes to my weight-loss journey, but I absolutely cannot wait to get there! The changes I have made to my lifestyle in the areas of fitness and nutrition are permanent lifestyle changes. Just like my career, this area of my life will never fully be *complete* because I desire to always be in the process of learning and growing when it comes to my physical health and overall well-being. Getting so close to my goal just once gave me a taste of what it's going to be like when I actually get there. I am going to complete *this* goal just like God has allowed me to accomplish so many other goals. I think the key to this is holding onto that belief and never letting go of seeing myself making it to the finish line.

It is not easy, so right now, the things I did along the way to motivate myself are coming in quite handy. I have a supportive life coach, a supportive personal trainer, and a supportive husband and family. I also have a large vision board devoted to my weight-loss goals, and I have journals and post-it notes with affirmations all around me to keep me laser focused on manifesting the experience I see myself having in this area of my life. I remain excited about what is to come!

Sometimes Things Get Scary

A LOT of people quit. We all know people who routinely start things but never finish. I know people who started writing books but never finished, started crocheting large blankets, but ended up with a few stitched rows and a ball of yarn tucked away in a closet. I know people who wanted to start businesses but never developed a business plan, who planned to earn a college degree but never took the first class or finished the final one... and so on, and so on, and so on. Unfortunately, we all know more people like that than people who follow through and reach their goals.

No matter how many times I have seen this, it still breaks my heart, but I know it always goes back to the student's initial mindset. This is the reason *how* you finish, and *if* you finish, are so strongly tied to how you started. Others can inspire you, but to finish, your motivation must come from within.

Those around you also reflect who you are, and they influence you (whether you want to admit it or not). If no one around you ever finishes anything they started; or if every person around you is a dreamer who never takes any actions and follows through, then that is a serious problem. It is problematic because it may likely be challenging for you to imagine *yourself* finishing your goal. It might also be challenging to gain the support you need around you to make it to the finish line because the people in your inner circle (although well-intentioned), will not have the experience necessary to know how to best support you.

I see it all the time with people who say they want to lose weight. Before I got serious about losing weight, I had never really been exposed to a community of people who knew about fitness and nutrition and who lived healthy lives at their ideal weights and were consistent about it. I have been intentional about positioning myself around supportive people who are winners. As a result, I now regularly see examples of real people living healthy lives grounded in self-care and overall wellness. Thankfully, this has now become my new *normal*. It is so important that people in the caterpillar stage have an opportunity to see other people reaching their goals. How else are those of us who reach our goals ever going to be sources of inspiration? How will we ever convince people to pursue their own goals? So, finishing your goal and achieving things in life is never just for you. It is always more than that. It is always bigger than that, and there's always more at stake. You never know who's watching. You never know who has noticed what you're pursuing and is pulling for you behind the scenes. You would be amazed at who needs to see you make it. Imagine the impact it will have on their lives when they see you reach your goal and live your dream. It will give them hope that they can do the same!

Sometimes things get very scary right before we hit that finish line. A feeling of "Oh, my God. This is really about to happen," kicks in. When that occurs, it usually creates one of two dynamics—a feeling of intense excitement and anticipation or a feeling of sheer terror. Either way, it is at this exact point along the journey when we must push through to completion, because the blessing is right around the corner. Finishing must be our only option.

I saw this with my current husband Alex when he was about a year into starting his own business.

Everything in Alex's life had prepared him to work as an outstanding employee for someone else, and he did exactly that successfully for various employers for more than 30 years. Then he got laid off during massive layoffs and decided to follow his passion for being a full-time personal trainer and competitive bodybuilder. I watched Alex transform into this new identity as an entrepreneur, and I saw those many times along the way when he considered giving up. He was doing everything he knew to do, but things were not happening as broadly or quickly as he had anticipated. There were many mornings during that time when Alex lay in bed next to me and talked about returning to the corporate world. That's not what he wanted to do, but he was afraid, and his fear was convincing him that he needed to take the safe way out.

I offered listening support and other encouragement during this time, but the ultimate decision had to come from Alex. Thankfully, he had begun his journey with a sound, disciplined mindset and a passion for helping people through fitness and nutrition. Today, thank God, Alex's business is flowing with clients and opportunities for him to grow and operate his business in a new realm. When he had no clients at all, he didn't realize that success was right around the corner. If he had given up, he would be back on a nine-to-five corporate IT job and not fulfilling God's purpose for his life.

We all know what giving up feels like. It does not feel good. It represents failure and is often associated with feelings of guilt and shame. Even if something must be delayed, I don't think giving up should ever be an option on the table. It is amazing what God can do, so there's no need for us to ever know *how* things are going to happen. We just need to flip our mindset, start our journey, and never stop until we get to the top of the mountain! I promise you, when you finish something, especially something that was very challenging, the view will be worth the climb... always!

Wing Tips

My Incredible Journey: Completion

- What do I look forward to about completing my goal?
- Who may likely still be around once the hardest parts are behind me?
- Who will be cheering me on to the very end?
- What will I do if I feel scared right before I finish?
- What type of support will I need to make it to the finish line?
- How will I know I'm done, that I've reached my goal?
- How will I celebrate my success?
- What goal will I pursue next?

SECTION V

PHASE FIVE:

The Butterfly

Butterflies are beautiful flying insects
with large scaly wings. They are very good fliers.
They have two pairs of large wings covered with
colorful, iridescent scales in overlapping rows.
Veins support the delicate wings
and nourish them with blood.

Breathless Preparation for Joy!

I wish I could bottle this feeling I have

Random acts of freedom

And forgiveness

And fear

Time

Standing

Still

In the midst of chaos

And uncertainty

Breathless preparation

For unknown joy

Toying with remembrance

Laughter

And dance

Chance heatings
And unwavering disdain for self
On the shelf

Forever

Peace apples and lollipop sunshine
Fateful
Grateful
Terrorizing
And amazing
So many beautiful things to see

A new beginning
No longer descending
Into handshake promises
Just plain

Pain

Those questions won't be answered today

This is not a goodbye poem
This is a hello, good morning, how are you poem
A good to see the new me poem

An arousal of self poem
A glow in the darkness with Light poem
A no more fight poem
A chance meeting for a new life poem

A where do we go from here poem
A happy from the inside out poem
A filled with joy and delight poem
A doing flips in the morning sunlight poem
A love, light and everything's gonna be alright poem

A soul poem

A heart poem

A now poem

A change poem

A life poem
A live your life poem

Go live your life

CHAPTER TEN

Gives Me Chills

*We had become a community,
a family of women coming out together very early every Saturday morning.*

I wish I could bottle the feeling I get when I dance. I have always loved to dance. I have never danced professionally or even taken professional dance classes. I'm just that person who hits the dance floor at the wedding receptions and moves like no one is looking. I don't have to have alcohol in my system in order to have fun on the dance floor, and I don't care who's watching. It's just one of the places where I feel most free and least inhibited. Believe me, it has nothing to do with my skill level.

Several years ago, a close friend invited me to attend a line dance class. Before I could decline, she said, "Just trust me. It's not what you think." The only thing I knew about line dance was the Electric Slide and what I saw on television in country western bars. So I went, mainly to appease my friend, and because I had recently divorced and was looking for healthy outlets—things to do.

My life has never been the same. I went to the class, which was held in a big open space inside a historical building on an island in the Lowcountry part of South Carolina. There were about ten people there and they all seemed to know each other, but were very friendly and welcoming. The instructor was a retired schoolteacher who had started this community of line dancers who met periodically (throughout each week) to learn new dances, get some exercise, and fellowship.

So, it turned out that "line dance" doesn't mean the same thing to everyone. This was a SOUL line dance class. That's right. All the dances we learned were for R&B, Motown, and some modern hip-hop songs. It was sooooo much fun! The instructor taught everything step-by-step, and she repeated it without the music until we caught on enough to try it with the music.

Of course, as with anything brand new, I didn't catch on perfectly at first, but I was having such a great time learning. The music was great and there was something special about moving all together in formation as a group. I absolutely LOVED soul line dancing. I kept going back each week, taking classes at least twice a week. Over time, I got to know the other students in the class, and I enjoyed welcoming first-timers.

I had become a regular, and I was fully involved in that local community of soul line dancers. We attended special events where we spent the entire weekend learning new dances with soul line dancers from the around the country. We would dance throughout the entire weekend (almost literally), from Friday until Sunday; and sometimes we took part in showcases where our group was one of the featured dance teams.

We also volunteered in the community, performing soul line dance formations in local parades and at places like the Boys and Girls Club. It was so positive, so healthy, so friendly, and just plain fun. It was inclusive of people of all races, all body sizes, and all ages. It gave me something to do that was also good for me and became another way to give back to others.

At one of those weekend-long events, the organizers offered a sort of pre-conference workshop where you could pay an extra fee and take a day-long class to get certified as a line dance instructor. I decided to do it and my friend did it with me. We learned everything we needed to know, and I eventually applied that knowledge by teaching line dance classes, from time to time, on the campus where I worked and at other special events.

A couple of years later, I accepted a job at a different college several hours away in another part of the state, where my husband and I currently live. It was hard to move away, and I seriously missed my soul line dance community, but thankfully there were a couple of active groups in the city where I moved. In fact, one of the best, nationally known soul line dance instructors and choreographers lives here. He is super engaged, and holds a weekly dance bootcamp, in addition to other events. However, I always wanted my own class.

I had a goal (a dream) of having my own class so I could build that same sense of community I had first experienced when I got involved in soul line dance. I'm not saying this sense of *special* doesn't already exist here; I just wanted to add to it. I wanted to bottle that feeling I get when I'm on the dance floor and pour it into others. I wanted to contribute to spreading this amazing fitness and fellowship opportunity to the world. I wanted to do my part to make sure it's available to anyone who wants to try, because it's something you can do at any age and any socioeconomic status. The more we move our bodies, the better our quality of life.

I had built a little teeny, tiny name for myself as one of the local soul line dance instructors, so I had enough of a following to generate some excitement about starting a new class. A local gym owner had a large, open group fitness space with a smooth floor and a large, full-wall mirror—the perfect environment for a group dance class. He also had a booming sound system, great parking, and all the other amenities that would ensure people would feel comfortable and be safe when they came for class.

So, I started a class! I did it! I promoted it with fliers, on social media, and by word of mouth. Our first class had over 40 people! That's a lot in the world of weekly soul line dance classes. I was in HEAVEN! My vision had become a reality. I had a room full of people of all ages, races, and backgrounds together in one big room DANCING. We danced, we laughed, we made mistakes, but it was all in the name of dance, fitness, and fun.

Week after week, people continued to come. I offered free cold bottles of water, fresh fruit, and other snacks. I sold tee shirts printed with our group's name, and each week I provided a handout with an inspirational quote.

We had become a community, a family of women coming out together very early every Saturday morning. Some people began to stay after class just to talk or open up about something going on in their lives. They helped me break things down and carry them to my car, and they started attending other soul line dance classes offered in town on other days. That is EXACTLY what I was hoping would happen—that we would begin to stitch ourselves together and become part of the fabric of the local dance community and start spreading the good news of soul line dance to others.

One of the highlights of my time with that group was when we all went together to a five-day soul line dance event. There, literally hundreds of other teams from the around the country had come to hang out, laugh, and just celebrate the joy of dancing together. There's just something that gives me chills when I see a room full of 300 people dancing together in formation with smiles on their faces and their hands in the air. It feels like the entire room is moving—like the earth is moving. It is just so powerful, rewarding, positive, and so healthy.

When you're doing something that brings you that much joy and a sense of freedom, you cannot help but get out there and share it with others. You have to soar!

CHAPTER ELEVEN

SOAR!

Success comes with many rewards, but it also comes with
the responsibility of sharing, giving back, and helping to clear the path for other people to live their dreams.

Ahhh... now we're getting to the part for which you have been waiting. This is what all the hard work and sacrifices are all about. This is the part of the transformation journey that makes it all worth it because you get to soar! When you are soaring, you have the feelings and experiences that confirm you are exactly where you are supposed to be, doing precisely what you are supposed to be doing.

This is the step where the former caterpillar (now a butterfly) lets go, leaps from her supportive branch, and SOARS! She is no longer climbing and clinging to support. She has reached the destination she had previously given herself permission to dream about in the beginning, even before she fully understood what it was like "up there." She just sensed it was something better than where she was… and now it's everything she thought it would be, and more.

She is colorful and beautiful. She has wings… WINGS! These new appendages open up a whole new life for her. She is now free to visit, explore, and have new experiences beyond her wildest imagination. She takes chances, makes new friends, and feels brand new.

Despite all that amazingness, here are some other things I learned about butterflies: there is a lot of pressure to maintain their wings and be beautiful and fly. Plus, it's tough out there among the other butterflies. In fact, in nature, if you look closely at butterflies, you'll often see their wings are nicked and torn because they have to fight. Things aren't always the way they seem from far away. It reminds me of one of my favorite sayings, "People see the glory, but don't know the story."

By no means does making it to the top and getting to the point of soaring mean your work is done. It means you now know *how* to succeed, but the work continues, because you still need to maintain yourself and protect your dream. You still have to exert a great deal of effort. The stressors and problems will be unfamiliar, and the battles you face will be different from what you experienced before, and they will be in new environments. Despite those things, you still won't want to go back to where you started. Would a butterfly ever dream of returning to life as a caterpillar? Think about that.

A Whole New View

Education, formal or otherwise, is one of the most powerful ways for a person to soar. Sometimes it comes with various forms of sacrifice—things like time, money and sleep. However, the beautiful thing about education is once you have it, no one can ever take it away from you. Once you have learned what you set out to learn, it will be yours forever. It is a permanent transformation that changes you from the inside out because it has the power to broaden your knowledge and alter your point of view.

There's something about learning new things that expands your mindset and ultimately your entire world. It can also affect the life trajectory of your family for generations to come. It is often the great equalizer in an otherwise inequitable world. Just as the butterfly can't go back to being a caterpillar, a person can't go from being educated back to uneducated.

Higher education changed me so much from the minute I started earning degrees. It wasn't even so much about what other people thought of me. Rather, it was more about how I began to think about myself. It felt good to work hard, make sacrifices, and finish something. It felt good to see things in new ways. It felt good to learn how to do things I had never previously considered, or never thought I would be able to do. I couldn't *unlearn* those things, and there seemed to be no limit to the opportunities and the ability to learn and apply more.

As a higher education practitioner, I am a professional who values, and often necessitates, certain levels of education to access particular career opportunities. With every degree I earned, a new entryway opened for me to fly through and soar.

Educators are literally in the transformation business, so it's important that we model what complete transformation looks like. I always remind myself that when people come to us to pursue degrees, the best people models are the people who believe and have proven results to show it can happen—because they have done it themselves. Transforming my life through education has put me in a position to help others in that way. For me, that's soaring!

It Could Only Have Been God

The feeling of soaring in my career has come at those times when the opportunities that came along could only have been sent by God. For example, within the past couple of years, I have had the chance to make an impact on higher education by serving on the Board of Trustees for an important national organization. I soar alongside university presidents and system chancellors—people in more advanced positions than myself. To this day, I have no idea who nominated me.

I was recently nominated to serve on the Executive Council for that same national board, and the agency head called me herself to notify and congratulate me. Wait? What? Me? Throughout so many of my transformations, I have seen God's hand at work. I have had experiences for which I didn't think I was ready, but He put me in a position where I had no choice but to leap off the branch, trust, let go, spread my wings, and fly.

I share all this to demonstrate for you that soaring requires wings, but it also requires ongoing courage. Continuously tapping into that courage is a part of the work that continues even after you have reached your goal.

The good news is we don't have to do it alone. God will send people to help us and nudge us into situations beyond our wildest dreams. We should just be open to it and remain ready to make the leap even when we're scared. That way, we can fly into a new realm where we will be able to utilize the gifts and talents God gave us.

Once You Go Butterfly, You'll Never Go Back

Once you experience this type of transformation, you no longer function as a caterpillar. Change of this magnitude often permanently affects how we show up in relationships. As caterpillars, we were okay crawling through experiences and accepting whatever was available to us at the bottom for survival. However, as butterflies, we know our value and expect to be treated properly and experience happy, healthy relationships.

Soaring in many areas of my life has absolutely affected the way I manage my relationships. For example, I more readily put myself first by doing something as simple as not answering the phone if it's not a good time for me. It doesn't mean I never help other people. It doesn't mean I never drop what I'm doing to help other people. It means I make better choices, and I factor my needs into those moments when I have a decision to make. That might seem small, but for me, those decisions represent my ability to value myself. I choose *me*. Have you ever heard the saying, "That's just how I roll?" Well, that's just how I soar!

Once I began to soar and operate in a new realm, I learned I could not have butterfly conversations with caterpillar people. So, I released friendships that were grounded in negativity, gossip, and judging. Don't get me wrong. I was fully involved in all those unhealthy habits and behaviors with them, but once I began to change, I became intentional about choosing to be around other people who are soaring—people who are full of energy, encouragement, spirituality, entrepreneurship, and fun! Those are the types of people I enjoy being around, and I try to be the same way and inspire others. We are all works in progress.

Romantic relationships are no different. I have never stopped believing in marriage and healthy relationships, and I always had the sense that there was supposed to be more for me in life... that God had something different in store for me. To experience *different*, I couldn't show up as a caterpillar. I had to trust, leap, and soar as a butterfly, ready to love again.

I was still getting used to my new wings when I initially started dating after my first marriage ended. I had only ever known how to be a caterpillar in a love relationship. As a result, I had a history of getting stepped on because I was rarely authentic, established very few boundaries, and had very low expectations of the people I allowed in my life. Of course, those early relationships did not go well at all.

However, I had grown enough through my other transformations to know my value and had developed new self-care skills. I had learned what soaring felt like in other areas of my life, so I knew being lied to and taken for granted were not things I had to tolerate to be liked or accepted by another person. I learned how to cut cords (or sometimes God cut the cord for me) and walk away quickly from bad relationships, without apology or much explanation. Just like my other transformations, I had a goal and needed to remain laser focused on it. My goal was simply to end up in a healthy relationship where I would be happy and able to exist as the healthiest version of myself, while adding value to the life of another person.

As a caterpillar, I would have never joined the online dating site where I met my husband. I would not have had the self-esteem or courage to put myself out there like that. Having experienced multiple forms of transformation, I anticipated eventual success, so I was willing to take action. I expected to experience the ups and downs that naturally occur with dating, and I did.

On a dating site, I had to engage with others in an authentic way and be friendly and outgoing. It also meant I needed to maintain boundaries, and I did all of that. I did not settle. I understood the value I would bring to a relationship with the right man, so I just entered the early friendship with my now husband as my regular self—flaws and all. Instead of trying to be impressive, I was open and honest about my past, my insecurities, and my feelings for him. I allowed myself to be vulnerable, and I didn't try to make myself small by minimizing my accomplishments and dreams. That was all new behavior for me, but I had to grow into it and learn from the experiences in my previous relationships. Over time, I grew and evolved in a way that made me ready for a healthy relationship in the covenant of marriage. That doesn't mean our relationship is perfect. There's no such thing. What it *does* mean is he is the perfect partner for ME. I did not have to lose myself to be in this relationship, yet I continue to have the space to grow and discover new parts of myself. As a life coach pointed out to me, "It just flows."

Most days, I feel such a deep sense of gratitude for knowing my life is on the right path for me—for what *I'm* supposed to learn and experience. It's okay to be happy. Just like the butterfly, I am no longer at the bottom like a caterpillar looking up. I still have work to do in this marriage and in all my relationships. I must get along with others, be courageous, and fight for what I need by setting boundaries and speaking up, even when it's scary.

It's Heart Work

Although I have not yet reached my ultimate weight-loss goal, I already feel like I'm soaring because I have experienced so many moments of pure joy and character development throughout the process. Getting healthy is truly the gift that keeps on giving, and I don't have to wait until I hit a final number on the scale to experience that. In fact, each time I hit a weight-loss goal, I experience the feeling of soaring. It is a high. It is one of the best feelings in the world because it is tied to something positive and healthy.

When you lose a lot of weight, your clothes no longer fit properly—and I'm talking about everything; undergarments, shoes, coats, jewelry, everything. It was fun to give away clothing that no longer fit and bless others with it. It was also fun to go out and purchase clothing in new sizes I hadn't worn in a long time, and in stores where I previously could not shop because they didn't carry my size.

Soaring!

The compliments from others also feel amazing. When people who haven't seen me in a long time, run into me and don't recognize me, that feels exhilarating. As wonderful as all those things are, the most rewarding feeling during my weight-loss journey has been reducing my medical risks and getting off blood pressure medication. That was empowering! I felt like I was sitting on top of the world, like I was floating. I told people about it, and I posted about it on social media. I wanted everyone to know they, too, could do it if they needed to. This was especially meaningful to me as an African American, because so many people in our community suffer from dangerous chronic diseases that we can avoid with lifestyle changes instead of manage with medication and costly surgical procedures.

I know part of the reason I am here on this earth is to show people they can do this, teach people *how* to do what seems impossible, and encourage them along the way. Everything happens for a reason, but losing weight, getting healthy, and making it to the finish line as the best version of myself has been life changing for me in a permanent, lasting way. It's also *heart* work because I genuinely want my achievement to inspire others into action and completion. The passion I feel has given me wings!

<u>Soaring Every Day!</u>

It breaks my heart to think that some people never get to soar. But it's also what drives me to share my story and the stories of others. My life has been defined by a series of successful transformations. Some have been easier than others, but one thing I truly know about myself is—I am a finisher! I am a person who knows what it feels like to push through and make it to the end. I want others to know what that feels like. I want people who have never seen or tasted success to experience it. I know once they do, they will want more.

Reaching goals and succeeding in life becomes addictive, but in a good way. Some people chase success for the power and influence that often comes with certain achievements. Power and influence are needed in many situations, but that's not what does it for me. I love the feeling of "I did it." I love the feeling of overcoming my fears and inspiring others in the process. I am addicted to setting goals and reaching them because doing so has always made my life better in some way, and I have never regretted trying.

The goals don't always have to be major, life-changing things either. It can be something as simple as getting out of bed thirty minutes earlier every morning to allow time for prayer, exercise, or meditation. It could be a goal to perfect a fancy cake you saw on a cooking show and want to learn how to make. Although goals like these may not seem as massive as a goal to graduate from medical school, the steps are still the same and the feelings of achieving those goals can be just as powerful.

For example, my brother owns a hot sauce company. Sometimes his goal is to develop and test three new flavor compositions over the course of a weekend. He gets such an incredible sense of satisfaction when Sunday evening comes, and he has three bottles of brand-new, exotic-flavored hot sauce ready for family and friends to beta test before he takes them to market.

So, when people approach you with questions about how you did it, answer them. When people seek your mentoring, say, "Yes." Be willing to support someone else just like people will have supported you along the way. Success comes with many rewards, but it also comes with the responsibility of sharing, giving back, and helping to clear the path for other people to live their dreams—no matter how big or small.

Through finishing and giving back, you also get to experience a sense of peace and purpose in your life. That is one of the most rewarding parts of soaring. I sustain that feeling through my faith—through worship, prayer time, personal devotional time, fellowship with like-minded Believers, and through personal reflection when I journal or just sit quietly and think. I recently added the practice of meditation. I found it to be quite challenging at first, but over time, it has become one way I am able to manage and appreciate silence and allow revelations to surface from deep within. Whatever works for you, the main thing is to find ways to maintain the feeling of peace and centeredness that accompanies the satisfaction of personal goal attainment.

In this book, I have focused on sharing about transformations in four areas of my life: education, career, relationship, and weight loss. In every single one of those situations, I have been blessed to experience what it feels like to soar. I give God all the glory for that because I could have had the same experiences without ever reaching that feeling of peace and purpose, that feeling of knowing it's my time to soar!

Wing Tips

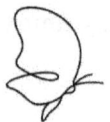

My Incredible Journey:

Soar!

- How do I imagine my life being different once I have achieved my goal?

- What behaviors or activities will I use to nurture the sense of peace and purpose I will have?

- How will I give back and help others who have similar goals.

CONCLUSION

Transformation

Butterflies undergo a complete metamorphosis
in which they go through different life stages...
a beautiful, flying adult butterfly emerges.
This adult will continue the cycle.

Red

This red suit made her feel fierce! They couldn't touch her when she wore it. From the moment she slid the straight, fitted skirt over her hips and allowed the hem to hit right above her knees, she felt that body language power and turned to the side to admire her hard work and God-given curvy goodness.

Side zipped.

She was all tucked in... smooth and secure, and you couldn't tell her nothin' with this new red everything underneath.

Good choice.

Fiercely red through and through... she always loved the way her body looked in lace, but a red lace bra? Shooooot!!

Perfume.

A little here, a little there, and her makeup was *fire*. She smiled a little at what she saw in the mirror, stepped into her shoes, and then practiced her presentation smile.

Perfect.

The jacket lay on the bed... smoothed out, waiting, knowing its role, its power as the finishing touch, the final transformation. That jacket would change her into a superhero—into the amazing woman she was. She picked it up and admired the smooth silk lining and slid it over her arms one at a time. The fabric-covered buttons added a subtle elegance, and each closed button further accented her waistline, offering modest coverage of her full bust.

She looked good... really good.

She smoothed the jacket in place with both hands and just stared at herself in the mirror. She felt her perfectly red lips begin to quiver.

But then she remembered who she had become.

And just smiled.

CHAPTER TWELVE

THE BUTTERFLY ON TOP

Don't let ANYONE talk you out of believing in yourself.
It's your time to do whatever YOU need to do to become the best version of yourself.

I hope this book has offered insight and practical information about the steps you must follow to transform any area of your life. We have talked about the five steps of The Butterfly Experience™ transformation model:

The Butterfly Experience

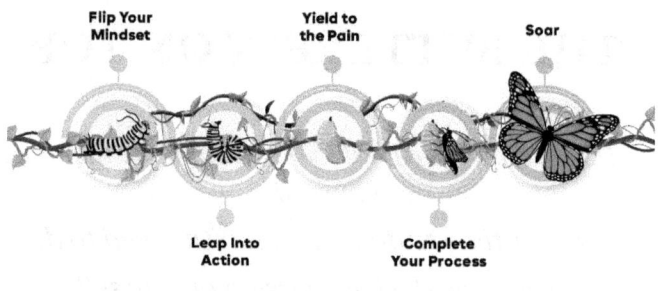

Flip Your Mindset

I shared personal examples of transformation in my own life in the areas of my education, career, relationships, and weight loss. In each of those situations, I had to change the way I saw myself. I had to change the people around me—removing some and adding others.

Leap Into Action

To make changes in my life, I had to *do* something, and sometimes the things I had to do were new and uncomfortable, but I did them anyhow.

Yield to the Pain

I never enjoyed the luxury of skipping any of the steps—especially the pain. There was always something incredibly uncomfortable about the process, even if the goal was something I desired. Going through the tough things so many times helped me understand what it takes to finish. Those experiences taught me how to understand tough times and benefit from those valley experiences instead of just suffering through them.

Complete Your Process

We talked about completion. Many people have difficult experiences while pursuing a goal, but most don't push through to the finish line. It's like driving through a storm. If you just keep driving, you will eventually get through it, and the sky will be clear and blue, allowing you to see where you were going all along. No storm lasts forever, but some people are in the habit of pulling the car over, stopping, getting out and living in the storm with no hope of conditions ever improving.

Soaring

Finally, we explored the concept of soaring and the feeling of peace and purpose that results from going after something, doing the work, hanging on when the going gets tough, and finishing. There's nothing like it. It doesn't matter if it's something grand or something small; the steps are the same. The things required of you are the same, and the amazing feeling at the end is the same.

I discussed the importance of going back and helping others once you have achieved your goal. It is a natural part of the process. Even if you have never viewed yourself as a mentor, you will find that people will seek you out. You'll also notice that you will want to help. You will feel so good that you will want others to know what it takes so they can feel just as good.

You must do the work. Period. If there are things you need to face in your life, face them. Get gritty and uncomfortable, and don't run from anything about your past that might be getting in the way of your progress. In fact, it's going to be there whether you deal with it or not. It is going to affect you whether you deal with it or not.

Keep in mind, there's no specific timeline for how long any type of transformation should take. It depends on the nature of the goal and your own readiness to navigate the steps. It does not matter, as long as things progress in a positive, forward, and upward direction.

Do not let ANYONE talk you out of believing in yourself. It's your time to do whatever YOU need to do to become the best version of yourself. That includes turning your *ordinary* into *extraordinary* and living a life where all your dreams become a reality.

It's Your Time to Soar!

"And be not conformed to this world:

but be ye transformed by the renewing of your mind,

that ye may prove what is that good, and acceptable,

and perfect, will of God."

Romans 12:2 (King James Version)

APPENDIX

DISCUSSION QUESTIONS

In the next few pages, I have provided some thought-provoking questions and prompts to help you get started in processing your thoughts.

I left a little space after each question so you may jot down anything that comes to mind right away, but I strongly recommend you seriously take your time, be honest with yourself, and write in a journal about whatever comes up for you as you think through each question.

It might also be powerful for you to discuss these items openly and honestly with an individual or group you trust. I hope you will find these tools helpful as you navigate your own journey.

1. I know the following beliefs are holding me back in certain areas of my life:

2. If I'm honest, those beliefs have affected the quality of my life in the following ways:

3. Do those beliefs fit with my values?

4. If I don't change these beliefs that have been holding me back, in ten years, my life will be:

5. To help shift my beliefs to support my goal, I will:

6. I really want to achieve my goal because:

7. When I think about my goal, I feel happy because:

8. In the past, I have been successful at:

9. Who do I trust? Who has been there for me in the past and would be there in the future?

10. What are some small things I can start doing right now to put me on track to achieve my goal?

11. How serious am I about this goal?

12. If I were not afraid, I would:

REFERENCES

Daniels, Jaret C. *Vibrant Butterflies: Our Favorite Visitors to Flowers and Gardens*. Adventure Publications, 2018.

Norris, Alores C. *I May Not Be Perfect, but My Lipstick Is*. House of Flawless, 2021.

ABOUT THE AUTHOR

The first in her family to earn a college degree, Dr. Knowles earned an Associate of Arts degree from Piedmont Technical College. She then went on to earn a Bachelor of Arts in Counseling and Human Services from Limestone College; a Master's in Career and Technology Education from Clemson; a Graduate Certificate in Higher Education Leadership from University of South Carolina; and a PhD in Higher Education Administration, also from the University of South Carolina.

Very active in the community, Dr. Knowles has served on numerous local and national civic and professional boards and is a member of multiple organizations focused on serving and supporting those who need it most.

Founder of MatteelSpeaks and a graduate of the legendary Les Brown's Power Voice System (a program for professional speakers), Dr. Knowles is a sought-after motivational speaker and workshop presenter. She performed a TED talk for TEDx Greenville in 2016 and continues to present regularly to all types of groups on a variety of topics designed to inspire those who desire to transform their lives.

Dr. Knowles currently resides in Greenville, South Carolina, with her husband, Alex Knowles.

For information, or to connect with Dr. Knowles, visit:

www.matteelspeaks.com

Instagram | Facebook | YouTube | LinkedIn | Twitter

-

www.ingramcontent.com/pod-product-compliance
Lightning Source LLC
Chambersburg PA
CBHW050108170426
43198CB00014B/2500